When Teachers are ready, their Students appear

A selection of essays and experiences of S. Quanaah

~Quanaah Publishing~

Quanaah Publishing

www.quanaah-publishing.com

When Teachers are ready,
their Students appear
©Copyright 2015
Quanaah Publishing

Written/Edited by S. Quanaah
Cover Design by S. Quanaah

-FOR TRAINING AND PUBLIC SPEAKING INFO-

S. Quanaah
EMAIL: atlantisbuild@gmail.com

www.atlantisschool.blogspot.com
www.youtube.com/quanaah
www.soundcloud.com/atlantisbuild

Printed in
The United States of America

Introduction

In a society where it is often expected for students to be properly prepared in order to learn, it must be equally emphasized that our educators are properly prepared to teach. This book is a series of essays pertaining to teaching Knowledge of Self [KOS] from the cultural perspective of a Five Percenter.

-S. Quanaah

A Quest For Fire

When I was in the second grade my teacher Mrs. Smith asked our class what we wanted to be when we grew up. Some said football players, others said doctors and still others said a lawyer. Of all things I could be I said, "I want to be a Zoologist!" At that age, and even today, I've been an animal lover and nature enthusiast. There wasn't a nature program or animal show I didn't watch and I would memorize their facts like some of my peers would do baseball stats. I longed to travel the world, study nature and narrate documentaries like Jacques Cousteau, Carl Sagan, Donald Johanson, George Page, Marty Stouffer and Sir David Attenborough. Later on I became a big fan of the late Steve Irwin. I credit my Ole Dad with orientating me this way because he sat down and watched all of these shows with some of my siblings and I. We also invested a lot of time on the Tuscarora Reservation in our area and through this socialization I became much more aware of my relationship to the planet. Besides the Cryptozoology, the study of hidden/mythical animals like big foot, loch-ness monster and etc. that many youth find fascinating, the core aspect of any animal study is animal sexuality, mating habits and their family dynamics. Have you ever seen leopard slugs mate?

Within that study of animal sexuality, mating habits and family dynamics exist the roles of being dominant or recessive - regardless if animals roam in packs, herds or live solitary. In other words, sexual prowess, the right to mate and ability to sire/birth offspring depends upon that animal's status, genetically, physiologically and socially. Those who are most dominant and hold the rank to do so are known as Alpha Males/Females. Those who are recessive and don't hold that rank are known as Beta Males/Females. Sometimes certain animals are born Alpha or Beta Males/Females and that is their fixed destiny. In some cases that isn't true. Take an orangutan for example. All orangutans don't have pie faces with those big meaty cheeks called a flange. Only "king orangutans" do -which is caused by a massive testosterone growth spurt similar to that of Dr. Bruce Banner changing into the Hulk. So in this sense, an orangutan that appears to be a Beta Male can transform into a mammoth Alpha in a matter of months. On the female side, a mating queen bee is dominant in a colony based upon her ability to reproduce -and there's always virgin queens killing off their sisters and waiting in the wings to run the Bey Hive. In this regard, we as humans are not much different, or better, than animals.

ALPHA — Will Smith in 'Hitch'
BETA — Ross in 'FRIENDS'
OMEGA — Seth Rogen in 'Knocked up'

This brings me to the discussion about Alpha vs. Beta human behavior, particularly among males. There are a host of websites that categorize the qualities and characteristics of males as either Alpha or Beta, dominant or recessive, masculine or feminine. The truth is ALL males possess Alpha and Beta male qualities -some more than others. ALL males have a little Alpha Tony Starks [Iron Man] and Beta Peter Parker [Spider Man] in him. I think the problem arises when we as males fail to recognize which qualities are the most appropriate to express in a certain situation. For example, known for being more aggressive, domineering, assertive, hot headed, primal and etc., an Alpha Male mentality may not be the best way to resolve some conflicts. In the same sense, the laid back, quiet, sensitive, peaceful and etc. Beta Male mindset may also not be the best approach to deal with some confrontations. Either of these approaches/dispositions may be right and exact today, yet totally wrong tomorrow; wisdom allows us to differentiate this. In a western society steeped in misogyny, male chauvinism and sexism, the John Wayne, James Bond, 50 Cent image of Alpha Males often takes precedence over the application of wisdom. Even worst, you have Beta and even Omega Males fronting, posturing, posing and aspiring to these non-contextualized western ideas. I see these males every day, or on social media, trying to convince people that they're #1 [Alpha]. This pissing contest competitiveness does nothing but perpetuate the low/vacant esteem and inferiority complexes these males are really dealing with. In the quest to be number #1, most males don't consider the fact that they already are, respectively, as the original man. This is one of the main reasons why some of my male peers find it difficult to "advocate a society of men or group of men for one common cause." This lacking is also what proceeds our inability to be equal, in everything, with each other. Some of us are so worried about thinking others are outdoing us, or trying to outdo each other, that we're not doing anything of real substance to uplift each other.

In the animal world, males typically demonstrate various forms of physiological pageantry to "show-off" their so-called dominance to each other and onlooking females. Whether it's flashing bright colors like golden-headed lion tamarins, butting heads like big horn sheep or singing sophisticated songs like a lyre bird, male animals, obviously in their primal state, thrive on competition. The same can be said for male humans -who have not evolved beyond our primal reptilian brain function. Cognitively speaking, there is no difference between a raging bull elephant during musth or a raging male talking bull at a parliament. Both are in the throws of passion and both are unreasonable. Aside from all of our pageantry and pheromones we give off to communicate our -genetic- profile, the most essential clue we share about that profile is our legacy. In other words, one of the main qualities a female looks for in a mate is security and all the showboating and Pherazone cologne in the world won't attract a female if we're insecure and we haven't secured a legacy.

Nowadays, as in our past, Ujima [collective work and responsibility] is one of the guiding principles of any group desiring freedom, justice and equality for and among its members. In order to carry this out successfully males in particular must be willing and able to cooperate. Cooperation is impossible if we're competing 'against' each other. I emphasis 'against' because I think competing 'with' each other is healthy -like we did in high school when our track team faced an opponent during a meet. If three of us were running the 100 meters, our goal was get first, second and third place for our team. There is no silver bullet when it comes to all of this yet the bullion consists of males being more honest with ourselves about where we're at, what we actually have and our commitment to brotherhood, family and community. One of the main reasons I have been and continue to be successful in my undertakings is because I'm not afraid to say I need assistance. I am also not afraid to not be the center of attention, top dog or quietly or loudly support a brother who is best qualified to represent a project, program or initiative. Some of us have a problem with that and it's this kind of pride that continues to come before our misfortune and destruction. We can act like we're money team members, take pictures with our chin up to look taller, thumb thug on social media or have sex with a different female every day of the week yet none of these things demonstrate manhood. Nor can we use any of that as practical tools to help propagate a family, communities or a nation.

American Horror Story: Asylum

Allah and Azreal

In May of 1965 after being arrested with several other men for unlawful assembly and disorderly conduct at a rally in front of the Hotel Theresa in Mecca [Harlem, NY], Allah [the Father] was arraigned in criminal court before Judge Francis X. O'Brien and held on a $9,500 bond. Four months later he was shipped off to the Psychiatric Unit at Bellevue Hospital. Allah would remain there until a final psychiatric report submitted to Judge O'Brien stated that "he did not understand the charges against him" thus remanding him to the NYS Department of Mental Hygiene for indefinite confinement. At the age of 37, Allah was confined in these institutions, Bellevue and Matteawan State Hosptial, for two years. Matteawan was a limbo for sadists; a living nightmare used to house people considered too dangerous for civilian institutions yet too ill for prison. It was during Allah's stay in Mattewan that he met and befriended a young 17 year old Caucasian transfer from Elmira State Penitentary named John Kennedy. Because Allah didn't represent a religious group he didn't have the constitutional protection of religious freedom in a court of law. There were always others who considered themselves a diety, yet because they claimed it within a religious context, they were afforded religious protection under the law. Allah was not afforded that protection and some Five Percenters are still being catagorized as 'criminally insane' and denied the right to practice our culture in correctional facilities around the country. Allah also wasn't politically affiliated, a member of any organizations or representing any institutions. Therefore, he didn't have their support, publically or privately. He stood alone, and as he came to learn, the 17 year old Caucasian boy he met in Matteawan stood out, and alone, in his own way too.

Allah and Azreal

Born on September 28th, 1948, 17 year old John Kennedy was Allah's first Caucasian student. As the first Caucasian Five Percenter, John adopted the name 'Azreal' becoming a prototypical model of how Caucasians were educated and entrusted to function within the context of our growing national body. As a civilized man who was empowered with the knowledge of his people, and ours, Azreal grew to educate people on how to survive and avoid the snares of this devilish society, especially mental health institutions. He had a lot to tell because he had been through hell. An institutional hell that he knew so well that Allah symbolically gave him the keys to it.

I knew Azreal personally and one of the things he always talked about is how he suffered in various facilities, especially Matteawan, because of his name. Some of us took that for granted and never looked further into what Azreal may have been striving to communicate. "Yes the President's name was John F. Kennedy and Azreal's birth name was John Kennedy" some of us thought, believing that Azreal was just proud to have an honorable name that many of our people looked at honorably. Well what politics and policies did President John F. Kennedy represent that the guards at Matteawan felt the need to persecute Azreal, AKA John Kennedy, for? Why the transference?

President John F. Kennedy

Doing further research I learned that John F. Kennedy spent his entire political career, as a Senator and as the President, striving to reform the mental health system. It personally hit close to home; his elder sister Rosemary was 23 when she had a lobotomy [brain surgery] that incapacitated her and eventually led to her death. In 1955, then Senator Kennedy sponsored the Mental Health Study Act to begin reevaluating the practices/procedures employed in mental health institutions around the country. As the President of the United States in 1963, President Kennedy authorized the Joint Commission on Mental Health to investigate mentally ill related problems and sponsored the Community Mental Health Centers Act to reform the entire mental health system. This final Act, was one month before his assassination. Following his death, in 1968 John F. Kennedy's sister Eunice Kennedy Striver, partially inspired by their sister Rosemary, started the Special Olympics.

Matteawan State Hospital

I mentioned an American Horror Story in regards to the mental health system because that's exactly what these institutions were, and Matteawan was considered the worst. Along with medical care that was below hospital standards, the institution's practices were barbaric; performing lobotomies and using shock/water therapy, hypnosis, sleep deprivation, starvation and other Spanish Inquisition-like procedures on people as young as their early teens. It's also worth noting that lobotomies were not carried out by professional surgeons nor were they performed in surgical laboratories. They were done in un-sanitized environments with poor lighting, poor staffing and crude instruments. This is not even mentioning the knuckle-therapy, sexual and verbal abuse people had to deal with or died dealing with while confined in these institutions where prison guards were also trained. It wasn't until the 1960's with the political pressure of President Kennedy, and during the time Allah and Azreal were in Matteawan, did the mental health system begin popularizing the use of psychotropic drugs for psychiatric treatment. However, this did not spell relief for these inhabitants of hell; the drug experimentation, overdoses and Thorazine straight jacket's made it that much easier to carry out the knuckle-therapy, sexual and verbal abuse.

No I am not saying or implying that Allah and Azreal were sexually abused. Because of the nature of the environment, both of them were verbally abused and Azreal talked extensively about the physical abuse he suffered. Allah, Azreal and others witnessed many of these things and lived to tell about it. Many who survived this hell still carry a mental diagnosis along with physical scars. All of them suffered some degree of **PTS** [Post Traumatic Stress], including Allah. Allah was confined there for two of the five years he and his companions organized the Five Percenters; that's 40% of the time he was here among us. Have you ever asked yourself why there's not much conversation about that time, or have you even considered how he was psychologically affected? As Five Percenters, some of us romanticize the idea that the Father showed and proved who he was and just walked out of Matteawan unaffected. Just researching the state of the mental health system in this country at the time Judge O'Brien deliberately remanded him to it would show you this idea is unrealistic. The state of this country's mental health industry was so horrific that John F. Kennedy, as a Senator and as the President, made its reformation a key talking point of his entire political career. One of his final talking points prior to his assassination. Given this history, it is my perspective that Azreal was more than a prototypical model of a Caucasian Five Percenter. He symbolized, in the name of John Kennedy, the reformation of the devil's mental health institution. With President Kennedy's Community Mental Health Centers Act he sought to de-institutionalize mental hospitals with community mental health services. This translated into the closing of long stay mental health institutions because of its reduced population, staff losing jobs and companies aligned with these institutions losing contracts [money]. President Kennedy was messing with a lot of people's money, which over time cut 90% of the beds at state mental institutions. Staff at Matteawan were forced to change and find a new hustle. They didn't like that, nor did they like Azreal's honorable name that represented that change. And because many couldn't reach President John F. Kennedy the President to show their dissatisfaction with these changes, they persecuted the John Kennedy they could reach. Azreal mentioned his honorable name, President Kennedy, the mental health industry and his experience in Matteawan often. He also talked a lot about Allah's compassion and insight to not only recognize what we was going through, but to educate him on how to become better. These correlations help us better understand the context of our plight as a Nation of Gods and Earths [Five Percenters].

After standing trial, Allah was eventually released from Matteawan in April of 1967. Some time after that Azreal was also released and came to Mecca to find him. Because of the national political pressure to change the psychiatric landscape of state mental institutions and the mental health industry as a whole, they, and others being held unreasonably, were able to go home. It wasn't because Allah debated a board of psychiatrists about the science of everything in life and they were so mezmerized by his wisdom that they just had to let him go. Nor did Azreal burst out of Matteawan like Chief in One Flew Over the Cockoo's Nest. Allah, like Azreal and others, didn't demonstrate the kind of maladaptive behavior, dependency or learned helplessness institutional staff documented to justify keeping them there. This was the climate of America during this time and slavery by another name; a 'citizen-to-asylum pipeline' that shuffled people into a system they often didn't survive.

In closing, keep in mind that nothing happens in a vacuum. Everything is not as explicit as we may like for it to be. Some things are implied, if we listen, and give us deeper insight and a better appreciation for what others may not say. Azreal and Allah found themselves caught up in a kind of system that many of us could only imagine. They, like many others, didn't walk out unscathed and there were things they saw and experienced that they probably took to their graves. So behind some of the things Azreal said, what Allah instructed some of us to do, and how they coped, is a story. A story that gives context to AWM.

Poverty is a Mindset

Who are the 10%?

Regardless how well intended and proficient Doctors may be, they are in the sick business. If they healed patients we would rarely need Doctors so they "treat" them instead -and the pharmaceutical companies are not mad about it. The same can be said about Lawyers; they are in the crime, personal injury and family dysfunction business. If it weren't for drugs, violence, accidents, divorces and etc., we would rarely need them too. I'm sure my barber is glad indestructible haircuts don't exist because if they did he would also be out of business. Whether we are mechanics, school teachers, dentists, politicians, pastors or etc., there's a certain degree of job security that comes along with fixing things or even striving to insure that things remain broke, as in "poor."

According to the 2014-2017 Community Health Assessment Niagara County Department of Health released in 2013, "23% of the people in our live below the poverty line and 44% of the population—almost one in two—is either in poverty or struggling financially and at risk." In Niagara Falls, approximately 60% of our residents receive public assistance such as food stamps, welfare, unemployment insurance and

Medicaid. According to 2009 data, 67% of the families in poverty are female headed households with no husband present, and 70% who are poor did not work. Another important statistic is that foreign-born residents are 94% above the poverty line.

When it comes to statistics, people can manipulate them to serve whatever political agenda they want. For example, in regards to 67% of the families in poverty being female headed households with no husband present, some people may simply say it's because they're not marriage material. Some people believe that the 70% who are poor, who did not work, are just lazy. The 94% foreign-born residents who are above the poverty line? Some may conclude they all work harder. Whatever statistics say, there's always an angle of what can be said, which is oftentimes inaccurate or disingenuous.

One of the misconceptions people tend to have about public assistance is that their taxes pay for it. In part, they do. All of us who work allocate a certain portion of our taxes towards supporting our public assistance program. The reality is Niagara County receives financial support from New York State and the Federal Government to fund our public assistance program. Because of the statistics related to poverty, and accompanying socioeconomic factors such as teenage pregnancy, poor education and etc., Niagara Falls receives a larger portion of that

State and Federal support. In other words, if the city of Niagara Falls were a person named Nia G. Falls, they would be living below the poverty line, receiving public assistance and parenting thousands of children.

Another misconception is that the face of welfare is "Lazy La'Shaniqua" who has 7 children by four baby daddies living in public housing. Actually, the largest portion of State and Federal support Niagara County and Niagara Falls receives for public assistance goes towards contracts, personnel, employee benefits and administrative services, not a welfare check. So the real face of welfare, or those benefiting most from our city's poverty, have more common names than La'Shaniqua. They are most likely home owners with a two income household that rarely live in the 14303 zip code. Do you get the picture?

We need more hands working, less finger pointing and the sober realization that fixing the things that are broke about our city requires a different mindset and multifaceted approach. In the process, we also can't be naive to believe that there aren't people invested in things remaining broke [poor]. There are - and they don't look like the broken.

Confederate Considerations

Have you ever considered that Confederate Flag waving may be more of a symbol of reconciliation than succession? Or that many southerners, and their northern kinfolk, still feel perpetually slighted by the United States Government? Well consider the fact that in the 1860's, after the Civil War, Congress enacted legislation that authorized the President to purchase "cemetery grounds" to be used as national cemeteries for soldiers who died in the service of the country. By "soldiers" it meant Union soldiers, not Confederate soldiers. Confederate soldiers could not be buried in national cemeteries, nor were they afforded any benefits from the United States Government. So those aren't Confederate soldier names engraved on Veteran's Memorials or Confederate soldiers being memorialized on Veteran's Day -a National Holiday. When the remains of Confederate soldiers were found on the battlefield lying near those of Union soldiers, the Union soldiers were removed, buried with honor and they'd leave the Confederates' bodies rotting in field. It was only because of the fear of disease spreading were their bodies put in temporary shallow graves and marked with wooden headboards for identification. And it wasn't until private women organizations, such as the Wake County Ladies Memorial Association in North Carolina, assumed the initial financial responsibility to remove these Confederates' and bury them in southern cemeteries. Keep in mind that because the Federal Government administrated this construction of these National Cemeteries, former Confederate States also paid for this. Between 1898 and 1968, the government added sections to the national cemetery to accommodate the graves of veterans from the Spanish-American War, World Wars I and II, the Korean War, and the Vietnam War. The cemetery's annex is located due north of the historic original 17-acre property. Today, more than 6,000 veterans lay at rest in the national cemetery and there are almost 4 million people, "non-Confederate" Veterans of every war and conflict, buried with honor in 147 national cemeteries on about 20,000 acres of land.

So here it is, after the Civil War ended, the United States Government buried and memorialized their own union soldiers, symbolically spit on the unmarked graves of their southern kinfolk, and then made them financially responsible for a large part of constructing national cemeteries they could not be buried in and monuments they couldn't be memorialized on. And to add further insult to injury, black veterans earned a place in the ground and name on these same memorial monuments. Some present day American patriots would simply say, "That's what rebels get!" Yeah, well do you really think that's fair and reconciliatory? What about the noble American idea of being charitable to the opposition? It's not like every Confederate soldier was a slaver, they fully understood what they were fighting for and they were unrelated to anyone up north; the Civil War was like the Hatfields and McCoy's. The McCoy's won and made the Hatfields pay for a large part of the clean-up, an elaborate cemetery and monuments for the McCoy veterans for generations. Rescue me if I'm wrong but that doesn't seem like the best way to heal open wounds and every year during Memorial Day, Veteran's Day and etc. this history is indirectly, or maybe directly, thrown in people's faces. Also, I'm sure some of you are aware that there are soldiers in ALL WARS, including the Civil War, who fought and died for a cause they didn't fully understand or oftentimes didn't agree with. Armies need bodies and sometimes that's exactly what people were.

One of the biggest tragedies is to see people overlook, minimize or trivialize that fact. Just because one of these soldiers died on what may be considered a losing side doesn't personally make such a soldier and/or their family treacherous traitors or losers. It also doesn't make the same kind of soldiers who survived on the other side winners. These soldiers who sacrifice[d] their life for a cause they don't/didn't understand or agree with reflects the same marginalized groups in America that have been historically losing lives regardless who is declared a winner in war. THAT lost of life should always be acknowledged.

The NU Black Student Union proudly sponsors a discussion of student organizing and activism, and viewing of the documentary *Fire in the Heartland*. The film will be introduced by Tom Grace, labor activist and casualty of the massacre at Kent State University. Discussion will be led by Danielle Judge and Lou Dejesus of the *Buffalo Anti Racism Coalition*.

Wednesday, March 25th at 6 PM in the Gallagher Center Multipurpose Room. Refreshments will be served.

In this respect, one of the reasons historical wounds remain open in America is its perpetual disrespect and lack of acknowledge for the dead. From those who have died from the genocide of our Indigenous People, Blacks who were brought here and enslaved [Maafa], Interment Camps of the Japanese, southern Americans after the Civil War, Immigrants in the 1900's and of course present day Middle Easterners/Muslims and Southeast Asians. I recently attended a viewing/discussion of the documentary Fire in the Heartland at Niagara University by its BSU. Fire in the Heartland is about the National Guard's murder/wounding of Kent State students [May 4 Massacre] and the history of student protests in America. One of the most reprehensible parts of this story was how Kent State and United State Government disrespectfully handling the deaths of the fours students and nine who were wounded -one who suffered permanent paralysis. President Nixon issued a statement which read in part, "This should remind us all once again that when dissent turns to violence it invites tragedy." The problem with his statement was that the protest on that day on May 4th was peaceful and there are images and file footage to prove that. It took nearly twenty years, the 1990's, to even erect some sort of Kent State Memorial in remembrance of this horrible incident and even then there was controversy. This, including the Jackson State Murders; where two students were shot and twelve wounded by the police as they peacefully protested the Vietnam War and United States invasion of Cambodia reflect a systemic attitude in America about death. The death of those who are not viewed as Americans. Fast forward to the incidents of violence by local/state/federal law enforcement agencies against protesters and the handling of the dead surrounding the Occupy Wall Street, Ferguson, Baltimore and etc. and you'll see this clear pattern.

150 years after the Civil War, there are some people who use the Confederate Flag as a symbol of hate and white supremacy. That is wrong and unfair. There are others who honestly look at this same flag as a symbolic reminder of their ancestors; some who died in a war they didn't fully understand or agree with, and others who use it a symbol of this country's lack of reconciliation/respect for the dead. Knowing this, it is likewise wrong and unfair to simply designate ALL Confederate soldiers, and their progeny, as treacherous traitors and losers. The Indigenous people, Africans, Immigrants, Women and the LGBT community are not the only people with an American Horror Story; some Southern Whites have one too. Lastly, the Confederate Flag, or any non-American flag be it the Rainbow, Jolly Roger, Pan-African, Christian, Nation of Islam or etc.., should not be flown over any city, county, state, government agency or public institution such as a public park, library or

school. None of those flags represent this nation, the United States of America, and should only be flown on/over one's private property or worn on their person. All of this begs the questions we can only answer for ourselves: When there is clear disrespect for the dead, how can there be respect for the living? If our ancestors are not buried [resting] in peace, how can we live in peace? All of us have family and friends who have passed away. Some of us may still be grieving behind their passing and how their burial was handled. Healing those wounds and bringing closure may require us to invest in a reinterment process; beginning with openly talking about that grief or feelings of disrespect and working together to strive to reconcile those issues.

Brand Ambassadors

In Search of Coretta Scott

Towards the end of the Summer I was having a very in depth conversation with a close female friend of mine. After explaining to her some of the things I deal with as a public figure, and the considerations/challenges that come along with finding a mate, she said something to me that was both hilarious and insightful in terms of compatibility. She said, "Dang, you sound like you're looking for Coretta Scott King."

Her statement made me reflect upon my past relationships in comparison to where I'm at today. In my teenage years the major qualities I looked for in a girl were how attractive, nice and smart she was. Of course this was before I had my first sexual encounters, and when I did.., this also became important to me. Two decades later, I never thought I'd be considering other qualities that are important to me when it comes to compatibility. Qualities that some of my contemporaries often don't understand because there are things I deal with that others don't have to consider. For example, this niche website now receives over 120,000 visitors a month. Although some of these visitors purchase my books/music via the links I provide, this traffic is primarily for the purpose of reading my articles.

This translates into emails, messages and inboxes I receive every day from people throughout the world for various reasons; which means a certain portion of my day, every day, is dedicated to following up with people who are reaching out to me. Mind you, this has nothing to do with correspondences I receive in the postage mail or my other social networks Youtube, Twitter, Facebook and even LinkedIn. Add the various initiatives/events I organize or participate in, my STYA youth program I facilitate in my local community, other projects I work on as a creative artist/book publisher and it gives you a partial glimpse of what my world entails. It's a lot, and sometimes feels overwhelming, yet I love what I do!

All of this got me to thinking about how my perspective of relationships has evolved to the point of seeing each other as Brand Ambassadors; someone who is capable of effectively representing your relationship [the brand] at home and abroad [nationally and internationally], in person or via their social media networks. Your brand is your mark, label, identity and what you represent. Therefore, when we're considering potential mates, dating/courting is really a rebranding process and how we're living is a graphic representation of that brand. Fresh off of the campaign trail running for public office in my City, I came upon an online discussion where women were talking about attire to wear at formal events. Some of them, although sweet, were totally inexperienced and didn't understand that flats/sandals or other accessories were inappropriate for such a venue; especially when your companion is the guest of honor where you may be called upon to say a few words. Although this may appear to some as a small thing, in terms of cultural competence, etiquette, social graces and the level of sophistication required to recognize certain social cues and navigate various environments, a woman like this would not be readily compatible for me, brand-wise. Consider if President Barack Obama had Joseline Hernandez (from Love and Hip Hop Atlanta) as his first lady instead of Michelle Obama as his Brand Ambassador... Sure she may be perfectly compatible with someone else, yet she is not presently compatible with The President of the United States [POTUS] for various reasons. Can she become compatible? Possibly, in time. Yet a POTUS doesn't have time, they have at least four years and that's a lot of public image/relations work and public scrutiny to deal with while striving to fulfill the duties of that Office.

Ironically, Dr. Martin Luther King Jr. chose a woman, who by her own account, was incompatible with him at the time of their marriage. As a young Coretta Scott, she aspired to be in the music industry and had no real interest in MLK or his future as a Minister when they met in College. Coretta wasn't smitten, she looked at Martin as short, literally, and in time he grew on her. Even months before their wedding day Coretta was still uncommitted to marrying him and confided these reservations in a letter to her elder sister Edythe. This wasn't a case of cold feet, she understandably didn't want to give up her promising career and become a Preacher's wife. So on their June 18th, 1953 wedding day, in which she had the vow "obey your husband" removed from the ceremony and retained her name "Scott", Coretta Scott-King reluctantly sacrificed her dream of becoming a classical singer and became MLK's Brand Ambassador. It was actually in the years following the death of her husband that she was brought to the forefront and became the face, political impetus and momentum to carry on the legacy of the Civil Rights Movement. She wasn't down from day one, she learned to love Martin and his mission. I mention this to illustrate that even Coretta Scott King, as notable and world renown as she is, was unresolved about her commitment to the brand. Today, with the proliferation of professional women asserting their autonomy and pursuing their careers, men are more likely to find women who will face this same dilemma when it comes to compatibility. And many of these women are remaining career women because they're not enountering men with an actual mission.

Keep in mind that everything I'm saying goes both ways! A woman should also consider if a man is capable of representing their brand at home and abroad [nationally and internationally], in person or via their social media networks. Sometimes I see brother's women leisurely post statuses/comments via social media that a woman by my side would get publicly burned at the stake for, but I have to remember, "That's their brand." Some people exist in a world where they only need to consider how their words/actions affect their family members, friends or co-workers because that's the extent of who they deal with and their sphere of influence. In my world I may get an email from France or South Africa about something I say/do or meet some random person who recognizes me in a different State/City who'll ask me about it. It has happened and happens so I have to consider differently what I say and do. I also have to consider differently how I respond to what people say and do against or in alliance with what I do.

You know, I've been intimate with women over the years, more often than I'd like to admit, yet as I've grown in my purpose I understand the level of responsibility, accountability and scrutiny that has come along with being a public figure. Even if we aren't, I think being responsible and accountable is important. I also understand that the women by my side will immediately inherit that responsibility, accountability, scrutiny and probably more so because 1.) How society defines females and 2.) The lens females assess each other through. It's a lot to deal with and in some cases I've only shared a part of my world with women in order to not burden them with everything I do. The more I shared, the more they learned they would have to share me with the world, and would ultimately be expected to speak for me in my temporary [schedule conflict/sickness] or definite [death] absence. Some women are simply not prepared to be an active part of a legacy and I've learned to accept that, sometimes reluctantly. The opposite is also true; some men are simply not prepared to be an active part of a legacy and women must learn to accept that. So No, respectfully, I am not looking for a Coretta Scott King. Although she grew to embrace his mission, Coretta was a career woman who wasn't looking for MLK and didn't recognize him, or his purpose, when she saw him. I am looking for someone different.

"It's not you, it's me"

For those of you who didn't know, I facilitate a youth mentor program called STYA which is an acronym for Successfully Transitioning Youth to Adolescence. My demographic are nine to twelve year old's and we do everything from critically analyze cartoons, arts & crafts, cooking classes and etc. to encourage them to expand their consciousness, build self esteem and discover their purpose in life as they transition into their teenage years. What I love most about working with youth, which I've done with various programs and initiatives for over a decade, is learning ideas, attitudes and behavior adults have in their infancy. In other words, I see nine year old girls learning to play the "make a boy jealous" game that eventually becomes a fully functioning operating system I see thirty something year old's use every day. Some things don't change, people just get older and continue doing the same thing. And the same way jealousy games may not change among females, some male's level of sophistication to appropriately respond to these games doesn't change either. I can't tell you how many times I've had to talk a ten year old boy down from an emotional ledge because some little girl was playing with his emotions. His reaction is no different than seeing emotionally unstable men committing social media seppuku because of what some female is, or isn't, posting on Facebook. Some of us simply never matured intellectually or emotionally; we're just older versions of the same child.

Because my Ole Earth was a Social Psychologist I've been orientated to analyze human behavior my entire life, literally. Normal family outings were going to places just to people watch; my Ole Earth would find a public place to sit with some of my siblings and I and we would discuss what we see in people's body language, style of dress and etc. One of the games she would also play with us was the book of questions -which I discovered later in life was a psychology book, not a game at all. This kind of investment into my growth and development as a child, coupled with the cultural contributions of my Ole Dad, has helped in my successful transition from boy to man. Some males never had a mother invested in them in this way nor did they have a father around to teach him what it means to be a man. Because of this, some of us have manufactured our idea of manhood 'a la carte' and the emotions and intellect surrounding this lacking remain raw, immature and underdeveloped. This is not an excuse, it's an assessment of what I've witnessed in its infancy and what it has the potential to become when it's not responsibly addressed as an adult. Ladies, young boys may destroy toys when they don't get their way. The same boy who doesn't get his way as a grown male, will destroy you. There's a lot of truth in what Drake says about b*tches these days.

Like with any group or society of people, some of its members are going to be emotionally and intellectual immature. One of the challenges I've dealt with over the years are these same boys/girls, not yet men/women, referring to themselves as Gods/Earths. Thankfully this doesn't reflect the overall consciousness of Five Percenters I know, yet there are some of us who are like that -sometimes for reasons only known to them. This is the reason I wrote the book Explorations of God/Earth

Mental Health; to empower my peers to recognize and address it. Because one of our cultural mottos is "Peace" or Positive Education Always Corrects Errors, we've always encouraged each other to grow and develop beyond whatever circumstance we've come from or are presently in. For any of us who are sincerely striving to elevate their consciousness and condition, it's a journey that involves removing the negative residue that comes along with seeing and believing ourselves to be inferior. All of us who have taken this step to gain KOS [Knowledge of Self] started out emotionally and intellectually immature. On many levels we're rewiring ourselves emotionally and intellectually and that takes work, sometimes a lifetime. Nothing happens over night, except the night -especially not the growth and development process.

In closing, I want to reiterate the importance of us men getting ourselves together. This is not to minimize the responsibility of grown females who need to grow up either. There are women I know who are successfully speaking from this perspective. As men, we can start getting ourselves together by being more vulnerable with one another by speaking honestly about our upbringing and emotions. I'm not talking about ranting, posturing or posting inappropriate stuff on social media under the guise of "keeping sh#t real"; that's immature and messy. I'm talking about investing the time to really examine who, what, when, where, how and why we think/behave the way we do with each other and the opposite sex. That is one of the most integral parts of KOS. Females share and are vulnerable with each other all the time. That female-to-female Educator and Student relationship directly, or indirectly, has remained pretty much intact since we've been in this country. Males are the one's usually holding stuff in and back from one another. Some of us males were grown up before we had an open conversation with men about hurt, lost, frustration, insecurities, inadequacies, embarrassing situations and etc. Even though some of us aren't sharing these things with each other in a healthy way, it always come out in the most unhealthy of ways -whether that's throwing tantrums or shade, being abusive, gossiping, broadcasting how great we are, taking serial selfies, being a whore or etc. Additionally, there are some things we've experienced as boys that we decided to take with us to our grave. Part of the emotional frustration or indifference you see us express is us trying to live with that lifelong decision. So ladies, when some grown males tell you, "It's not you, it's me", believe it! Also believe the likelihood that they haven't said or done anything about it for over twenty something years and don't plan on saying or doing anything about it after telling you that. We got work to do in order to help get our families/communities back in order and emotional instability and intellectual immaturity won't get us there. As civilized men who advocate righteousness, as Five Percenters and definitely as Gods, we must expect more from ourselves, and each other, to get that job done.

Waist-To-Hip Ratios

~*The Circumference of the Planet Earth*~

In Western Society the aesthetic standard of female beauty has always been blond hair blue eyes. Over the years that has somewhat changed -with women of color and ethnically ambiguous prototypes being marginally promoted as the new face of beauty. What has not changed much is the idea of body type beauty.

For over two decades Caucasian scientists have been formally trying to quantify a standard of body type beauty and came up with a waist-to-hip ratio standard to justify it. I say "formally" because Caucasians have informally entertained this idea body type beauty for many years prior to the research done by evolutionary psychologist Devendra Singh in 1993. One of their most notable fixations being Hottentot Venus [Saartjie

Baartman] -the archetype of Europe's crinoline, bustle, corset and girdle fashion eras. This is also where the notion of 36-24-36 body type measurement's come from. It was discovered via Singh's research that the ideal waist-hip ratio [WHR] for attractive females was a 0.7 WHR. In other words, if you measure your waist, and divide it by the measurement of your hips, that will tell you your WHR. This research was conducted on male populations from different cultural backgrounds and it was discovered that there has a consistent affinity for female's with a curvy figure where the waist is significantly narrower than the hips. According to the Journal of Biological Psychology Waist "Hip size indicates pelvic size and the amount of additional fat storage that can be used as a source of energy. Waist size conveys information such as current reproductive status or health status in westernized societies with no risk of seasonal lack of food, the waist, conveying information about fecundity and health status, will be more important than hip size for assessing a female's attractiveness."

This is one of the reasons you also see some models contorting their bodies in magazine spreads, photo shoots, music videos or exaggeratedly swaying their hips as they walk the runway. They're not simply posing. They're 0.7 WHR posers -giving you the illusion that they're more attractive than what they naturally are. And in this technological age, females get

Photoshopped to reshape/redefine their waistline all the time. That, my friends, is one of the subtle sciences of catfishing.

In addition to the blond hair blue eye prototype, the "woman with curves" standard of female beauty is also changing. Not simply because of a male's desire for a different aesthetic but the changing roles of female's within society and the hormone shift that has come along with it. Androgens, hormones that includes testosterone and is the precursor to estrogen, increase WHR ratios in a female by increasing abdominal fat. Excessive levels of Androgens cause a variety of symptoms including acne, weight gain, excessive hair growth, menstrual dysfunction and infertility. Cortisol, a hormone that helps the body deal with stress and regulate metabolism also increases fat around the waist. What this means can be summarized by Elizabeth Cashdan of the University of Utah:

"*Waist-to-hip ratio may indeed be a useful signal to men, then, but whether men prefer a [waist-to-hip ratio] associated with lower or higher androgen/estrogen ratios (or value them equally) should depend on the degree to which they want their mates to be strong, tough, economically successful and politically competitive.*"

In other words, a combination of diet, roles females have begun to take on within Western society and the accompanying stressors has begun to increase their production of Androgens, change Cortisol levels and ultimately reshape/redefine their WHR. On one hand this has increased the strength, stamina, aggression and competitiveness for females to meet the many socioeconomic changes within society -as female headed households, mompreneurs and corporate women have become common. At the same time and on the negative side, when this increase becomes a hormonal imbalance, it translates into one of the leading causes of poor fertility.

What does all of this mean? That there's much science to back the notion that we are in the age of true Warrior Queens; women of color and ethnically ambiguous prototypes that don't look like Marilyn Monroe and don't fit into one of her archetypal body casts. As I type this there still remains a white supremacist fight to hold her aesthetic standard of beauty on a pedestal. Just recently Vogue Paris featured its first black woman on a cover in five years. That says alot -in light of the historical/classical love affair the French have always had with women of color. It's important for us to reinforce the idea that our women shouldn't covet white skin and another woman's 0.7 WHR to be attractive. They, without that complexion and/or body type, are the true standard of normalcy and beauty around the world. Not because males have aesthetically declared it, but because the stability and destiny of our human family needs it. Our women must be reminded that they are absolutely fine the way that they are and their health, cultural contributions and commitment to our families and community is what our world needs more than ever before.

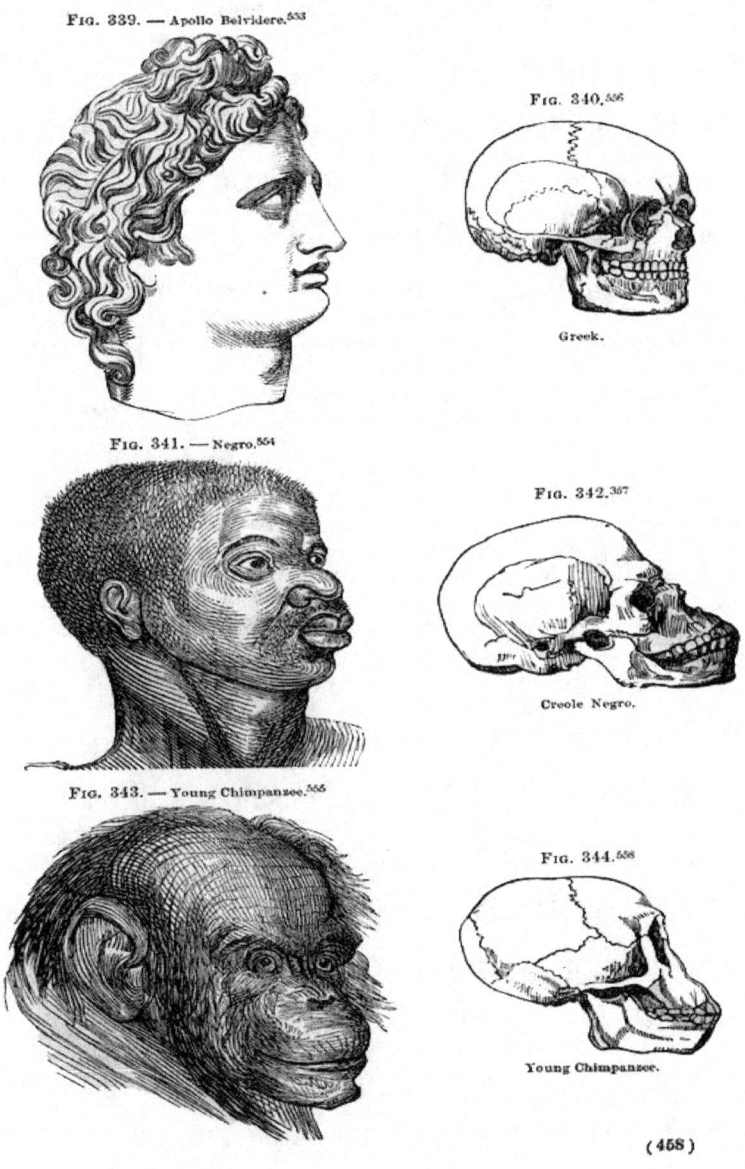

Fig. 339. — Apollo Belvidere.[553]

Fig. 340.[556]

Greek.

Fig. 341. — Negro.[554]

Fig. 342.[357]

Creole Negro.

Fig. 343. — Young Chimpanzee.[555]

Fig. 344.[556]

Young Chimpanzee.

(458)

The Amazing Race

~Part 1~

Growing up I dated various types of girls. Whether their ethnic status or nationality was so-called African-American, Italian, Haitian, Eritrean, Egyptian, Punjabi, German, Arabian, Puerto Rican, Greek, Native American, Jamaican and etc... I also dated various types of girls of different social statuses. Looking back on these experiences, I am thankful of the lessons I've learned along the way; some good, some bad, and yes, some ugly. As I matured I modified my perspective of relationships - realizing that I had to be more mindful of the challenges, conflicts and consequences that forging certain unions would bring. Many of us often have a "love is love", "love knows no color" and "everything will be alright" attitude when we enter our relationships and eventually find out that it takes much more than these flighty feelings to actually sustain it. In America, regardless what kind of relationship we have, racism always plays a direct/indirect role in that relationship. Realizing this, it's important that we take responsibility for how we allow that direct/indirect role to shape our relationships. I'm not just talking about being responsible for our personal feelings/gratification. I'm talking about being responsible for what our relationship, and potential family unit, brings into the world -especially children. No child is born a racist. Children are taught to be racists, directly/indirectly, by adults.

What is Race? The codified concept of 'race' can be traced back to a white Anthropologist named Earnest Albert Hooton. In addition to helping establish Harvard as the center for Physical Anthropology in the United States, Hooton was responsible for classifying human beings into groups and subgroups based upon phenotype (physical characteristics/traits); race. Through what is called 'comparative anatomy', Hooton used white people as the primary model of man and classified/defined black and brown people as primitives according to that basic standard. Based upon Hooton's work, in 1926 The American Association of Physical Anthropology and the National Research Council organized a committee to focus on the anatomy of black people (so-called Negroes at the time). A year later in 1927, the committee endorsed a comparison of African babies with young apes. If that wasn't enough, about 10 years later in 1937, the committee published findings in the American Journal of Physical Anthropology to prove, not suggest or imply, that Negroes were closer to primitives than the white race. Racial stereotypes about black intellectual inferiority, criminality, promiscuity, homeliness, amorality, socioeconomic ineptness, etc... are all associations with the pseudoscience of Earnest Albert Hooton. Although many white people already entertained/advocated these ideas and feelings about black and brown people for hundreds of years prior to Hooton's anatomical comparisons, Hooton was instrumental in classifying and systematizing these ideas/feelings into a framework that we've come to know and define as race -and ultimately racism. Even though Hooton was not a hood wearing, card carrying member of The KKK, who were already about 3 million strong in America approaching the 1930's, his work served as ammunition to advocate their White Supremacist philosophies, politics, and policies.

So here in America, this purely sociopolitical construct called 'race' was used as a tool to establish, justify and reinforce the power relations between people classified as white and others.

These power relations established a status quo; where the dominant society and ruling class is white and black and brown people, the minority within their society, are the underclass. Thus whenever white and black and brown people lived in proximity to eachother, the white group or ruling class controlled the institutions, political networks, finances, material resources and intellectual property. Even though whites are the minority throughout the planet earth, how can you explain these power relations that defy all logic and probability? Is this minority in control because it's just the natural order of things? Do black and brown people (the global majority) believe they aren't intelligent enough to govern so white people are better equipped to control the institutions, political networks, finances, material resources and intellectual property? Is there a systemic sociopolitical way of doing things that has empowered the global minority to gain control over the institutions, political networks, finances, material resources and intellectual property? And if there does exist a systemic sociopolitical way of doing things, has this been beneficial for all people, especially the majority? It is my perspective that the concept of race (along with 'racism' and 'sexism'), the sociopolitical arm of white supremacy, is one of the primary tools being used to accomplish this goal.

See, to even use the word 'race' in regards to human beings, we automatically "enter" (inter-racial) or "buy" into (bi-racial) the power dynamics that was propagated by the ruling class (white people) and codified by Earnest Albert Hooton's classifications. To consider yourself as a race, it automatically compromises your identity because the term race neutralizes/minimizes your ethnic/genus origin, cultural consciousness and nationality. As a person of color, it puts you on the primitive end of a categorical chart designed to uphold a dominant Eurocentric status quo. It's interesting to note that the findings of The American Association of Physical Anthropology and the National Research Council in the mid 1920's coincides with the proliferation of Marcus Garvey's UNIA (United Negro Improvement Association) and the founding of Noble Drew Ali's MSTA (Moorish Science Temple of America). The significance of this is the fact that Marcus Garvey and Noble Drew Ali advocated the importance of black and brown people's ethnic/genus origin, cultural consciousness and nationality. As a Nationalist, Noble Drew Ali even went as far as to instruct his members to learn 'The Color of Law" -used by racists to carry out racial inequality/discriminatory policies and procedures within the so-called justice system. This Ethnogenesis, advocated by the UNIA, MSTA, NOI, Five Percenters and other organizations was a vehicle to redefine ourselves outside of the white supremacist perimeters of race and within the context of our own ethnic/genus, cultural consciousness and nationality. Of course this did little to change the dominant society we were living under as a subgroup, or the sentiments of this ruling class. To undermine the progress of organizations like this, the ruling class began to promote the repackaging of 'race' under the pseudonyms of Colored, Afro-American and African American in order to get black people to continue entering/buying into a racist (racial) sociopolitical construct. The last and greatest ploy being bio-political subjugation via Interracial (enter 'race') or Biracial (bi-'racial') arrangements. How and what can be done?

The Amazing Race

~Part 2~

Interracial and **Bi**racial (**Inter**: *to enter into*, **Bi**: *to buy*)

As I stated in The Amazing Race Part 1, the words "interracial" and "biracial" are terms derived from the root word and concept of race. As I've expressed, race is an erroneous and pseudoscientific term used to classify groups of people based upon physical characteristics. These physical characteristics were/are used for the purpose to categorize the intellectual, biological, psychological, social and economic behaviors of these groups in order to reinforce the position and power of a ruling class and white supremacy. An example of this are some of the 'Criminology' theories of Earnest Albert Hooton that suggests that criminal behavior is linked to physically inherited characteristics; racist theories that still appear as a rule of thumb on the 11 o'clock news today. See: Crime and the Man (*Hooton, 1939*) When it came to Hooton's Criminology theories, the only problem white people had with them is when he started profiling white characteristics as criminal and inherently violent. Because his theories contradicted the status quo, white scientists began to go on record to debunk what Hooton proposed when it put white people in a negative light.

Let me reiterate that regardless what kind of relationship we have in America, racism always plays a direct/indirect role in that relationship. There is no way around that reality. There is also no way around the fact that America is historically race conscious and the dominant society (ruling class) are white people. Those of us who are black and brown are a subgroup (minority underclass) within their society. So the designation of relationships by 'race' (interracial/biracial) serves the purpose of reinforcing these power relations between white and black and brown people. It was through the concept of race that white people placed themselves in a dominant/superior position and relegated black and brown people to a recessive/inferior position. It was also through race that black and brown people, although collectively the global majority, have been divided and categorized into groups/subgroups of second class, third world citizenship throughout the planet earth; making it easier for the global minority (white people) to rule. So to be in an arrangement that is classified as "inter"-racial means a couple has knowingly/unknowingly "entered" the worldview of the ruling class thus upholding that status quo. To be in a "bi"-racial arrangement or even to call a child from that type of union "bi"-racial means a couple has knowingly/unknowingly "bought into" and "buys into" the supremacist worldview of the ruling class, thus upholding that status quo. Although this couple may believe this arrangement is equal because of their shared feelings, it does not change the reality that one person (white) still represents the superior or ruling class, and the other person (black or brown) still represents the inferior or underclass. These power dynamics are still institutionally evident in every aspect of American life and were never designed to be equal. They were designed to keep the ruling class in a socioeconomic position that's superior and another class of people as inferior and subservient to that class. See: The Help.

If I invented a Game and then invited you to participate in it, it's still my Game and you can only play according to my rules. So regardless if you call it interracial or biracial, by definition, that arrangement can only serve the purpose of reinforcing the status of the ruling class because they invented the Game of race. Regardless how equal such an arrangement is said to be, it's taking place within a society dominated by a white American way and that translates into home field advantage for the home team; the white person in that arrangement -regardless how humble, coy or meek that white person chooses to behave. If any problems arise, there will be no confusion about where this arrangement is taking place, who's the home team and who ultimately has the institutional power to control or dissolve that arrangement at will. Again, since black and brown people didn't codify the concept of race, and represent the subgroup/minority in any racial matters, we are a fundamental disadvantage. Looking at this Game of race, all arrangements, defined as interracial/biracial, serve the socioeconomic purpose of reinforcing and perpetuating the status quo of the dominant society or ruling class. It is also my position that the only way an arrangement like this can ever become a relationship that establishes true freedom, justice and socioeconomic equality outside of this status quo and ruling class bias, is that it must take place on the ethnic, culturally conscious and nationalistic terms of the black and brown person. In other words, the black and brown person must have home field advantage and their terms must be the central focus and primary foundation of that relationship -not the dominant society or ruling class. This, of course, is a very scary reality for any white person to honestly consider or accept because they come from a societal worldview where being the shot callers, having white skin privileges, their religious iconography, economic elitism and military might has always been considered the norm. As a matter of fact, less than 50 years ago, there were laws enforced all over America that banned black and brown people from even marrying into the dominant society and assimilating into the ruling class. This means that for 189 years of America's 239 year existence, or almost 80% of the time during the country's existence, black and brown people were restricted from legally 'entering' (inter-racial) or 'buying' (bi-racial) stock in the American Dream via any relationship with white people. Now honestly ask yourself, how can 189 years (almost 80%) of America's political policies, institutions, educational curriculum's, economic investments and religious teachings/iconography about black and brown people not matter now and have no influence on race based [interracial/biracial] relationships today? Even though these things were consistently implemented and reinforced by the ruling class for almost several generations, did their affect upon society and it's treatment towards it's underclass or subgroups (minorities) vanish in less than 50 years?

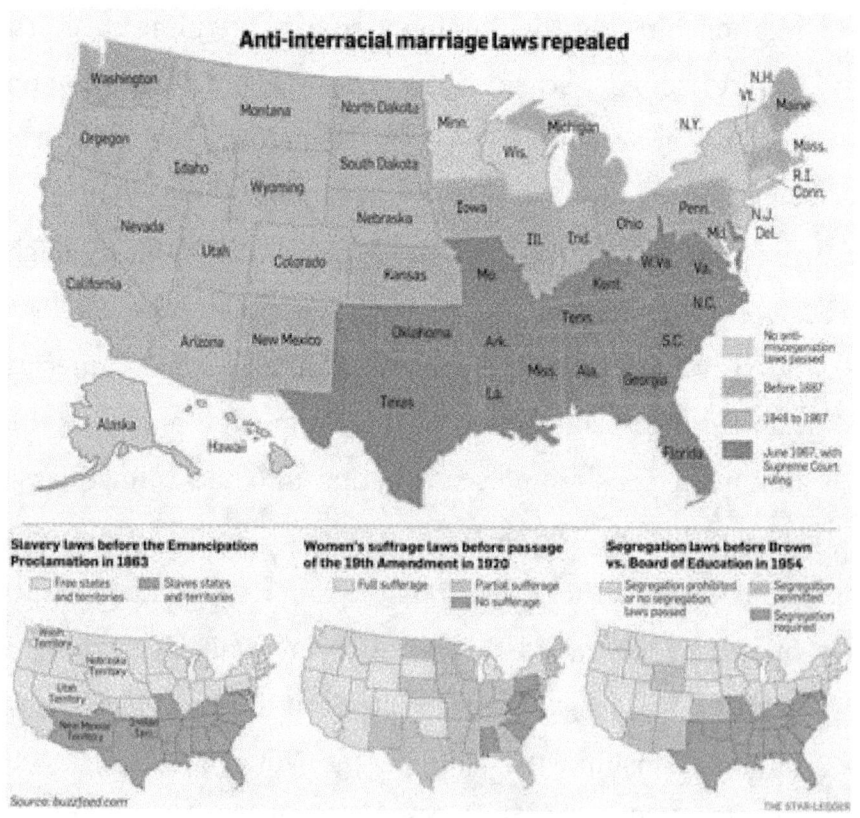

A common theme you'll always notice in any black and brown movement/organization seeking to redefine ourselves outside of the perimeters of race, is our association with ethnicity/genus (color), cultural consciousness and nationality as our worldview. It was understood that when black and brown people "enter" or "buy" into interracial/biracial arrangements, they must partially or completely abandon their sense of ethnicity, cultural consciousness and nationality in order to assimilate and identify themselves -generically- with the dominant society or ruling class. They identify themselves generically because any ethnicity/genus (color), cultural consciousness and nationality that doesn't represent the status quo is in opposition to the ruling class. So black and brown people who have bought into this Game will begin to espouse generic phrases such as "love knows no color", "we're all human", "we all bleed the same", "love is love", "love is blind", "color doesn't matter", "we are all dark when the lights go out" and etc in the interest of assimilating with the dominant society and avoiding a confrontation with that ruling class. What most black and brown people playing this Game don't realize is that identifying themselves generically and abandoning their sense of ethnicity/genus (color), cultural consciousness and nationality does nothing to address or equalize the power relations of the structurally bias arrangement they're in. As a matter of fact, it only serves to further empower the person who represents the dominant society or ruling class. How? Because the white person did not give up anything, and aren't required to give up anything, in regards to their status quo the black or brown person just "entered" (inter-racial) and "bought into" (bi-racial). They aren't required to give up anything because they are the home team; the standard model upon which all black and brown people are anatomically compared. Therefore, their standard model, and all of their Eurocentric trimmings, remains the foundation of that arrangement a black or brown person agreed to be a part of. In other words, in order to have an interracial/biracial arrangement, a black and brown person is required to leave most if not all of their ethnicity/genus (color), cultural consciousness and nationality at the door. This is the reason why you'll find the majority of interracial/biracial couples saying, "we are all the same" but still advocating standardized Eurocentric cultural values (holidays, religious rites, diets, clothing styles, social norms and etc.). This is also the reason you'll rarely cee interracial/biracial couples saying, "we are all the same" and openly advocating black and brown cultural values (holidays, religious rites, diets, clothing styles, social norms and etc.) and actively supporting black and brown movements designed to change the white supremacist status quo and position/power of the ruling class.

So for the obvious reasons I've stated, black and brown movements that are truly dedicated to changing the structurally bias status quo of the dominant society and position/power of this ruling class, do not advocate interracial/biracial arrangements. As Five Percenters specifically, we take it a step further and advocate relationships that are pro-righteous/civilized and anti-devilish/uncivilized. We don't classify the human family by race. We classify the human family according to ethnicity/genus (color), cultural consciousness and nationality. Regardless of this classification, what people choose to do in regards to themselves, their relationships with other members of the human family and their relationship with the environment is what ultimately determines if they're pro-righteous/civilized or anti-devilish/uncivilized. Those white people who have the courage, integrity, humility, studiousness and sincerity to learn how to embrace our culture, in order to educate their own people about what needs to be done to change the structurally bias status quo of the ruling class are not 'Gods' or 'Earths'. God, and the Earth, were already present millions of years before albinized (non-melaninated) people even existed. So because these white people strive for righteousness, they're respected as Five Percenters; citizens in our Nation who are respected as righteous/civilized members of the human family based upon their deeds. We are not pro-black, or anti-white because our worldview is not racially motivated -yet we know and understand that the dominant society has historically promoted a pro-white and anti-black and brown agenda. We are also not idealistic about white people taking on the gigantic responsibility of denouncing ALL OF THE BENEFITS that came/come along with being a categorical member of the dominant society and ruling class just to be a righteous man/woman. We recognize how unreasonable it is to expect most of them to give up white skinned privilege, family inheritance, quit the family business, share inaccessible information/resources with black and brown people and ultimately put their (and their family's) life on the line to establish socioeconomic equality. As a human family, there are certain biological, intellectual, socioeconomic, educational and etc. investments we are required to make that will not reinforce/uphold the status quo of the dominant society and ruling class. In love, there are certain types of relationships we absolutely cannot engage in. Our ideas about justice, civility and reformation cannot involve people who are invested in upholding an unjust status quo. Partnerships in business can't be made with people who feel/believe they are above the law. Also, accepting any terms that translate into usury, ignorance or being kept apart from another's socioeconomic equality is completely out of the question -which is historically an institutional reality for black and brown people who represent the minority and underclass in America and throughout the planet where there has been colonialism. In our worldview, black and brown people are first class citizens; first world people who fathered and mothered civilization. The average white person finds this extremely difficult to accept because it completely contradicts what they've been erroneously taught about themselves, and what they've seen around them, their entire life. Those white people who do bear witness to this truth are not the average; they're the elite among the ruling class. They represent members of the scientific, corporate, historical, political and medical community who secretly acknowledge who black and brown people are behind the closed doors of their masonic lodges and shrines (temples). And even though they have some of this information, they're not utilizing their institutions, finances, material resources and intellectual property to change or equalize the status quo between white and black and brown people. They were allowed to learn this information in order to be upright and noble, yet consistently fail to keep and obey the laws.

In conclusion, it's important to recognize and understand the power relations of any kind of arrangement -especially a relationship based upon the false concept of race in a historically racist (and sexist) society like America. If you're a black and brown person who's interested in someone who's classified as white, you need to assess/define that potential relationship along ethnic/genus (color), culturally conscious and nationalistic lines. This is important because it automatically reveals the power relations that you'll be agreeing to; maybe until death do you part! You need to know this white person's considerations and stances on issues concerning the minority subgroup and underclass this society put you in. Since white people represent the dominant society you live in, and ruling class you're under, you need to know their actual positions about slavery, sexism, lynchings, segregation, foreign policies, stereotypes and the present condition of the so-called race or subgroup of people you actually belong to; whether you choose to identify yourself with that so-called race or subgroup or not. See: O.J. Simpson, Michael Jackson, Kobe Bryant and Tiger Woods. When I say stances, I'm not talking about politically correct sympathy conversation about how wrong these things were/are. I'm talking about what they're actually doing about it. If they never did anything, or aren't doing anything, then they're upholding the status quo. Now that they've been made aware of these things, you have the opportunity to see what they're going to do about being in society's socioeconomic driver's seat. Some people will argue that you can't do anything about changing the past... Well what you can do is make sure what negatively happened in the past isn't happening in the present and doesn't happen in the future -starting with you, how you're raising you're children, and the people, places and things you choose to invest in. For those of you who want to act like this doesn't really matter, it does not change the reality of the status quo you're living under. I think it's obvious that people who are in so-called interracial/biracial arrangements may truly "believe" in a world of freedom, justice and socioeconomic equality, even if it's just in a bedroom. I also think that the thought of a world of freedom, justice and socioeconomic equality is a seed of a very noble cause. Yet until people can openly and honestly bring their ethnic/genus (color), culturally conscious and nationalistic concerns to the table and discuss a relationship (not an arrangement) based upon the power relations this relationship will establish, they're only co-signing the status quo of the dominant society and ruling class. As a black and brown person, your participation in such a structurally bias arrangement is not only a disadvantage, it's highly likely that you will suffer some form of psychological, social, financial and physical abuse at the hand of the person who represents the dominant society and ruling class. How is this possible? Because "who you are" as a minority subgroup and underclass in this society is not being considered. You're an after thought, if a thought at all. You're minority concerns are not primary, a priority, and usually irrelevant to the person who represents the dominant society and ruling class. While you have been forced through cultural assimilation to know and respect who they are, those who represent the ruling class have never been forced to know you. Therefore, it's impossible to have a healthy sense of respect, consideration and even love for who/what you actually don't know. Can you see how the person not being considered can get hurt in this situation? I can. It also makes one consider the self esteem and sadomasochistic/masochistic tendencies of someone who pursues structurally bias arrangements like this. In their mind, it Hurts So Good.

Now for those of you black and brown people who've already made this interracial/biracial decision without taking the time to actually think about what you were actually doing, you have two choices: 1.) Live with the complications you've accepted. 2.) Appeal to your white companion about renegotiating the structurally bias arrangements you've accepted along ethnic/genus (color), culturally conscious and nationalistic terms to make it fair. Good Luck because it's ultimately up to them, a representative of the dominant society/ruling class, to consider if your appeal is valid or not. Like with any relationship, growth is important. The challenge with any relationship based upon race, whether we're with someone we consider the same "race" or we call it "interracial" or "biracial", it's taking place on a racist white supremacist backdrop. There is no way around, under, above or through that. Our relationship, and family unit, must be willing and able to transform this ugly reality through everyday people activities that don't reinforce the status quo. Our acceptance or rejection of this personal and collective responsibility will determine that kind of world our children will inherit.

Are We Culturally Congruent?

Based upon my experience of formally having KOS [Knowledge of Self] 20 years September 30th, 2015, one of the biggest misconceptions I've seen people have about Five Percenter culture is that growth and development happens over night. In this fast food microwave society people often have the unrealistic expectation of "instant results." The reality is, nothing happens over night but the night and it takes years, months and days to unlearn and learn things that will improve our way of life and make us resourceful to others. Culture is not something we add water to, stir up and bake for 45 minutes. Culture is not something we simply read on this blog, nod our heads to in a cipher or listen to on Instagram clips. Culture is the sum total of all of our people activities which includes everything from our diet, language, the way we behave in private/public, our perspectives on education and economics and even how we define our sex life. Culture encompasses every aspect of our way of life.

When I first got KOS I wanted 120 Lessons. That is what I thought and believed was what it meant to be a Five Percenter; to know your lessons. While this is an integral part of learning the core values, principles, chronology, social norms and etc. of the Five Percent, I learned over time through walking with my Enlightener/Educator that lessons were not the sum total of this way of life. Over the course of our journey I also learned the Supreme Mathematics, our Nation's chronology, the Supreme Alphabet, Twelve Jewels and other sciences of life. Still then, these components which comprise our cultural curriculum were still not the sum total of this way of life. It took me years, months and days of experience to realize that regardless of our personal growth and development or individual accomplishments, they mean very little without the context of family and community -the cultural building blocks of any nation. In other words, in order to have a culture or sum total of people activities we must have a group reality; people. That sense of collectivism provides the context of culture because in order to improve, tend to, raise or grow anything it requires interdependence. In our physical environment that interdependence or network of organisms interacting together is called an Ecosystem. When it comes to us personally, without that sense of collective consciousness and sensibility, our way of life begins to reflect more of an Egosystem.

What inspired me to write this are the experiences of different people reaching out to me for support. One of the common things I hear is that Five Percenters in certain areas are not actively involved in their communities or doing anything for others. Aside from putting pictures and video clips on Instragram or being universal flagged-out on Facebook, many of these people are simply going to work everyday, if they are employed, and possibly attending a nation function once a month dressed in their Sunday's best. That is disappointing. That was not what the Father or his companions did. If that would have been the case none of us would be here because nothing would have been shared. I met my Enlightener unenrolled in a semester of college still going to physics, sociology classes and etc. to learn. That wasn't a typo, I said "UNENROLLED" meaning; he did not have to be there yet he was there to teach others. Some of us only take a class or training when it's necessary or we're getting paid. There are some Five Percenters who only engage the public, and other Five Percenters, monetarily. The only things they're ever involved in benefits them personally, including their own household, and they don't facilitate anything that solely helps others. That is a problem. Why? Because imagine where we would be if the Father had that kind of self serving mentality. Imagine if the Father and his companions' main platform was to monetize their relationships with the youth, their peers and anyone who looked towards them for guidance and support. Consider how it effects the lives of those in need today when the only time some of us are willing to do something, or ask others for something, is when it personally benefits us and ours?

This year I became an active member of a grassroots organization in my city called Niagara Falls Forward; a group of like-minded citizens invested in enhancing the quality of life for citizens in our city. Some of the things we've done are information sessions, a voter registration drive, food/clothing giveaways and we recently held our First Annual Niagara Falls Forward Family Festival on July 4th. Everything we've done has been made possible by the community, for the community. A couple of weeks ago we participated in a local event called Pints4Progress. Pints4Progress is an event held once month where citizens come together to eat, drink, socialize and vote on a project that will help improve our city. Each new attendee pays $5 and former attendee pays $10 to attend. With their entrance fee they get a meal/drink and after everyone has had a chance to socialize, several attendees are invited to present a five-minute project idea to the group. Once all those interested have pitched their ideas, each attendee votes on the project idea they favored the most, with the highest vote-getter taking home all funds collected at the door. The week we attended there were almost 150 people, seven presenters and I did a five-minute presentation about our First Annual Niagara Falls Forward Family Festival. We won the pot and walked away with about $1,300. One of the things I emphasized to the group is that although we would like their vote to help us secure a couple of bounce houses and other things for the children during our festival, we came to offer our help as volunteers for any of the businesses/organizations who were in need, and we came to ask if any of the attendees were willing/able to be a Niagara Falls Forward volunteer at any of our events/initiatives. We actually accomplished all three goals! One of the things I realized from this experience, that reaffirms some of things I've written about in this article and have reiterated over the years in my writings/videos, is that people are often more willing to help you help others than help you help yourself. Let me repeat that, "people are often more willing to help you help others than help you help yourself." Some of the other presenters who didn't win wanted people to vote for them to take the money to support their [personal] business. Yes I'm a strong advocate of localism, supporting black businesses and etc. yet that approach is no different than asking someone to take money out of their pocket and put it in yours. There's no magic, marketing scheme, bells and whistles website or infomercial to it. All it takes is the willingness and ability to do for others, period. This is something I consistently strive to communicate to others, especially my Universal Family, who are genuinely committed to successfully assisting others. Our First Annual Niagara Falls Forward Family Festival was very successful as well; we were able to serve over almost 400 people, had a basketball tournament sponsored by the WNY Elite Basketball Club, had three bounce houses for our children and gave away free ice cream and food -all which was made possible via sponsors and volunteers.

In closing, keep in mind that 'you are because we are.' Without the contributions of others, even the invention of something as unassuming as toilet paper, there are choices and opportunities we wouldn't have right now. The survival of any culture hinges upon its ability to cultivate human beings into a group of people who forge unions/units that share common attitudes, interests and goals. These unions/units become communities; the cultural framework for all of its people activities. The more we're willing/able to look out for each other, the less we have to lookout for each other. As Five Percenters, we should expect more of ourselves than functioning like a social club. Handing someone supreme mathematics or getting them to recite lessons does not make them an upstanding member of their family or productive member of their community. Our primary role as civilized people is to teach civilization, which is not just knowledge, wisdom, understanding, culture, refinement and not being a savage in the pursuit of happiness. Civilization is a group's advancement process in all aspects of their people activities. To grow and advance as a collective this means its people are tending to and raising each other up. The reason there are any positive advances or growth amongst any group of people it's because there are those, often small in number, who know and understand this. Our culture is not about what we can take to advance ourselves personally. Our culture is about what we're actually giving, each and every day in each and every way, to advance the lives of others.

Battle Royal

Meek Mill vs. Drake

When the media coverage of Meek Mill vs. Drake first went viral it excited me! Not as a fan of their work but as a lyricist, poet and outright music enthusiast. This moment put the focus back on lyrics. The last time the mainstream or general public were really interested and concerned about what someone had to actually say was that BET cipher verse by Kendrick Lamar when he put the entire industry on notice. To this day NO ONE has reasonably responded to that. Do you know who truly listens, dissects and critically analyzes rhymes regardless to whom or what? Rap Enthusiasts who genuinely appreciate lyrics, poets/spoken word artists, battle rappers and emcees/femcees. Last week 85% of the mainstream audience were just bobbin' their head to beats.

Another thing that I appreciate about this situation is it's potentiality to bring out the best lyrical content of artists. Busy Bee Starski vs. Kool Moe Dee, LL Cool J vs. Canibus, Jay-Z vs. Nas, KRS One vs. MC Shan, Ice Cube vs. Common and etc. are all instances where artists came with their best. As long as it doesn't go waaaaay left on some government co-opted Tupac/Biggie scenario it's a healthy landmark moment for Hip Hop in general and rap music specifically. Something else I've considered is its economic stimulus. The peripheral memes, videos, vintage tees, product placement and co-signs that not only generates web traffic but creates commerce is important. When Drake dropped his second Meek diss track Back To Back he used a picture of forgotten "World Series Hero" Joe Carter after hitting a three run homer to beat the Philadelphia Phillies. We would be naïve to believe that people didn't go out and buy Joe Carter paraphernalia that day? Brilliant! Drake also made good on his lyrics by sending Charlemagne 6 bottles of Dom P.. That was dope yet imagine if he would used his celebrity to get behind an up and coming entrepreneur and support their brand of alcohol by sending it to Charlemagne. What if Meek Mill responded by talking about charity work he's done for the Blackstone Foundation Library in Toronto? Personally I would love to see instances like this used to better empower everyday people and support local businesses.

After all of this Meek Mill finally came back with his response entitled Wanna Know which was wack from my perspective. His words weren't clear, Funk Flex added his theatrical explosions, there were samples and anything else you can imagine that distracts a listener. Although many people, including Philadelphians, expected more I still appreciate this moment in Hip Hop. Politically speaking it's no different than lobby groups putting the pressure on public officials to respond to a current situation. In rap music, people, not necessarily artists, oftentimes don't have this kind of pressure on them -especially when they're mainstream [Top 40]. Therefore, they say, do and sell whatever they want to the public. In this instance the lobby groups were everyday people using social media and hashtags to call for a response and we got one. Some may not realize this power to social economically engineer events and the growing political consciousness of the people but it is happening.

Almost three decades ago The Cosby Show highlighted an upper middle-class African-American family living in Brooklyn in the beginning of the golden era of Hip Hop. Yet the first time the culture was explicitly addressed/introduced was on a Season 2 Episode when the children were in the studio with Stevie Wonder and he sampled their voices and produced a beat with a synclavier. This was 1986 when Run DMC, Just Ice, Salt and Pepa, Steady B, The Beastie Boys, Afrika Bambaataa, Doug E. Fresh, Whodini, Too Short and others were making their mark within the chronology of rap music. At this time rap was still mocked as "jungle music", marginally accepted and Stevie Wonder served as an ambassador for a sound, creative process and exposure to a culture that would ultimately reshape the world. We have come a long way from this mainstream moment of time. Now it's common to hear some element of Hip Hop culture in every facet of television and radio globally. It doesn't mean that it's accepted, it means that there are people who are financially useful. We cannot overlook, minimize or trivialize that.

Some people have called this Meek Mill vs. Drake media coverage boring, overrated, wack, a distraction and etc. Yet the irony of this is the fact that they still found themselves commenting about it. That's like an Atheist talking about there is no God. At the end of the day, whether we like Drake, Meek Mill, Nicki Minaj's neutrality, this is a teachable/educational moment. If you're a Hip Hophistorian, use it as an opportunity teach others about the chronology of rap battles. Take a moment to educate yourself, and others, about "ghost writing" and one of the most prolific one's Smokey Robinson. Are you a rapper/emcee? Well make your own response to the situation or state of rap music. Do you make custom tees, a producer, graphic artist or etc.? Do something with Joe Carter or others such as Meek Mill's sister who has over 1 million youtube views in 48 hours. Find something of value in this that is inspiring, empowering and educational as opposed to just complaining. Add-on!

The Black Church

When it comes to GOD, my Cultural Worldview is what I choose to subscribe to. As a Person who is a part of a Group of People who subscribe to this Perspective, we are not in the business of converting, convincing, or coercing People to cee things our way. We are not Religious nor are we Missionaries. We are Civilized People who encourage eachother and others to be studious, discover answers for themselves and take nothing on face value -including what we share and know to be an actual fact. We respect and teach tolerance for other People's Religious/Cultural Worldviews and we won't allow/accept other People using their Religious/Cultural Worldviews to disrespect or be intolerant of us. This, of course, is the more "mature" way in which our Culture is expressed when we're dealing with People who have different Religious/Cultural Worldviews. Keep in Mind that this "mature" expression of our Culture IS NOT a reflection of everyone who considers themselves a part of our Group (The NGE). While some People are growing/developing at their own rate there are others who aren't and have no intention to grow or develop. I'm sure anyone can understand and appreciate this; ceeing that these same immature elements also exist in their own Religious/Cultural Community.

When I was young, unsure, and still striving to solidify my Cultural Worldview, I did quite a bit of debating and challenging others Religious/Cultural Worldviews. It was an exercise of Egocentricity and not much came out of those encounters. These weren't "dialogues" or "intellectual discourses" between People sharing Perspectives to learn from one another. These were battles to prove who's right, who's wrong and to show who had superior Knowledge; immature behavior you expect to cee from children, NOT Adults... -smh- Even to this day, People still strive to bait me into one these "Us vs Them", "Me vs You" Jousting Matches, b.u.t. I'm much wiser about involving myself in these Games nowaday. While speaking on the subject of Jousting, one of the biggest targets I'm ceeing within the so-called Conscious Community continues to be The Black Church and Christianity as a whole. I definitely understand and can appreciate the "Theological" concerns many People -particulary Black/Non-White People- have about Christianity, b.u.t. the outright disrespect for The Black Church itself, and someone's Belief System, I do not support or agree with. This is why...

Historically speaking, The Black Church has been and continues to be "The First", "The Oldest" and one of the only Black Institutions Black People still have here in America. During the Reconstruction Period in this Country AFTER Black

People were legally freed from Slavery, The Black Church served as a Socioeconomic 'Sawmill' that helped us establish, build, and rebuild our Communities. One such example of this rebuilding process was the central role the Mt. Zion Baptist Church played after the May 31st, 1921 Tulsa Race Riot burnt our Historic Black Wallstreet down to the ground. Even though this newly erected Institution was completed only a year earlier, after being destroyed by Whites during the Riot, the Congregation came together to rebuild it from the smoldering ashes it was left in. The Black Church was central to all of our people activities and reinforced our Ethics, Principles/Values, Social Norms/Mores, and Codes of Conduct. When Segregation was imposed upon us as a People, it was through The Black Church that we established a Support System/Network to produce Cultural Think Tanks, Educational Institutions, Businesses, Sports/Entertainment, Social Organizations, Social Clubs, Civil Rights Groups, and etc.. These Socioeconomic Entities did more than help us survive, they helped us THRIVE as a Group of People! When it comes to Social Norms/Mores, many of us wouldn't even know what 'Courting' is/was if it wasn't for our Church-going Elders down South! It was through the Black Church that we first learned forms of social responsibility/etiquette: like tending to the needs of the most vulnerable among us (our children, the mentally/physically disabled and our elders). In the Black Church we learned the importance of fairness, collective work and responsibility, respect for Family, chastity, and simply looking out for one another as a People. During these perilous times when America legally relegated our People to Second Class Citizenship and the Klu Klux Klan's Membership hovered around 3 million, it was The Black Church that became the Proverbial "Village" it took to protect and raise (grow & develop) the children who birthed the future generations of our People who are here today! It's a huge oversight for any of our People to minimize, criticize, or satirize this long-standing Legacy of our People and the undeniable contributions The Black Church has made to produce many of the privileges we enjoy today. ANY PROGRESS (Morally/Ethically, Entrepreneurism, Community Activism and etc..) that we've ever made as a Group of People in America either directly involves or has some indirect association with The Black Church. There is no way to get around this fact.

The biggest issue we cee with The Black Church today is, generally speaking and with some exceptions, it no longer functions as the socioeconomic nucleus of the Black Community. When "legal" Segregation ended in the 1965, many Black People started to "believe" we had all of these options and began to Integrate into a Society that never wanted us to be a part of it, by Law, for the last 189 years. Integration meant the Disintegration of many of our Black Think Tanks, Educational

Institutions, Businesses, Sports/Entertainment, Social Organizations, Social Clubs, Civil Rights Groups and ultimately the Socioeconomic Influence/Integrity of The Black Church. Today, in 2011, when we're looking at the variety of Black Churches around this Country, whether storefronts or mega churches, we're looking at shadows of it's former self... In my estimation, the dissatisfaction that alot of my People have with The Black Church today is a form of 'Transference' that's often expressed as a Theological issue. The true source of much of our dissatisfaction is the lack of love, respect, comradery, and support we have for eachother today. So beneath the dissatisfaction, there's a general sense of disappointment, sadness, and even depression because we're missing eachother and the sense of Community we once shared as a Group of People; a sense of Community that once revolved around The Black Church. Is this entirely the fault of The Black Church? I hardly believe that! As a matter of fact, there's a reason many People in Church, especially our Elders who remember the times when we depended on eachother, say, "Sweety when you coming back to Church?" If you take the opportunity to actually listen to them, and their experiences, I'm sure you'll find out that it's not a "Theological" request... It's much more than that.

In conclusion, THIS IS NOT an Article about encouraging our People who no longer go to Church to go back to Church. This is an Article to address the ignorance and oftentimes blatant disrespect I cee that many of my People have for our own Legacy! Recognizing the Legacy and Socioeconomic Function of The Black Church in America is a very important part of our past, present and future. Because many of The Black Churches today, no longer function as the nucleus of our Community, many People have lost their faith and support in this Institution. Many Black Churches often reinforce these sentiments because instead of functioning as the great luminary that was once central to our Community, they promote elitism, materialism, individuality, and separatism from anyone who doesn't believe as they do. Since my Ole Dad is friends with many Pastors/Deacons from different Churches within my City, at one point he approached them with the idea of them all utilizing the same Banking Institution to centralize/maximize our Economic strength as a People. Through this simple move, he said we could demand better Mortgage Rates, Business Loans, and etc... to help support our Interests and Building of our own Communities. This was many years ago and still hasn't happened.

This Article is about the importance of building bridges, working together as a People, and advocating for the same common cause; Socioeconomic Empowerment. Although we all may not share the same Theological Views, one thing we have in common is our Legacy as a People. Just because I'm not at a Church, Mosque, Synagogue, or etc... every Week DOES NOT MEAN that I'm totally against the Religious/Cultural Worldview some of my People subscribe to. I'm actually for the best of whatever these Religious/Cultural Worldviews have to offer in regards to empowering us as a People. When it comes to the Religion of Christianity, some not all, of its core teachings/customs are derived from our Classical Civilizations - particularly Hebrew Culture. Many of our People have a misconception that Christianity was beat into "ALL" of our People as slaves and that's historically untrue! While some were definitely coerced/forced to accept a Christian Theology, many of our People were wise enough to recognize that many of Christianity's core Teachings/Customs derived from our Classical Civilizations, and they openly embraced it. One such Man was Henry Highland Garnet; a 27 year old Presbyterian Pastor who delivered a fiery 1843 Speech Calling for a Slave Rebellion. Another such Christian Man was my Great-Great-Great Grandfather, a Minister, Josiah Henson; who escaped Slavery by taking his Family along the Underground Railroad up into Dresden Ontario Canada. In Dresden, Rev. Josiah Henson went on to survey and negotiate for the land to help found an entire Community, teach Financial Literacy, the Bible and establish a Educational/Vocational School called The British-American Institute. Here's his Self Written Biography. Another unsung Hero amongst the many Men and Women who came out of the Church to fight for the rights of our People was Dr. Vernon Johns; Dr. Martin Luther King Jr's Predecessor, Civil Right Leader and Brainchild of the Bus Boycott.

I, like any Civilized Person, am against the slandering, petty debating, and mud slinging antics I cee many of my People engaging in because of our various Perspectives of GOD - especially Adults who consider themselves Conscious who should know a lot better than that! Instead of actually Building (relationships) many of us are more interested in and even take pride in Destroying (relationships) by making mockery of someone else's Religious/Cultural Worldviews. There is nothing Righteous, Glorious, or Supreme about that; it's actually uncivil and oftentimes barbaric! The bottom line to all of this is that we need eachother, always have and always will. We need eachother today, just like we needed eachother yesterday, and WE CANNOT ALLOW petty differences to keep getting in the way and stopping us from serving eachother's needs; our survival and prosperity depends upon it. Regardless what Perspective we have of GOD (Divinity), it means nothing if we lack the will/ability to share that Perspective of GOD (Divinity) through how we treat one another. So I encourage all of us to refrain from all of this American Gladiator Mentality and begin thinking about ways we can work together to help bring an end to the crime, alcohol/drug addiction, amorality, homelessness, hunger, mis-education, poverty, family dysfunction, juvenile delinquency, and etc. that continues to plague our Communities REGARDLESS what Perspective of GOD we have! It wasn't The Black Church that put us in this condition, b.u.t. it's the sense of Unity/Community, which The Black Church successfully demonstrated, that kept many of us out of that condition.

The Mysticism of Sound and Music

The Emerald Tablet

The above image is soundtrack I released entitled "The Emerald Tablet." Since its release I've received quite a few questions about it and this article will answer these questions and share some insight into my reasoning/inspiration behind this Project.

Why is it called "The Emerald Tablet"?

Well to give you alittle background: In Esoteric or Occult Circles, "The Emerald Tablet" is considered a sacred book said to have been written by the Neter (Deity) Tehuti of Ancient Khamit/Khemet (Egypt) or from the Ancient Masters of the Lost City of Atlantis. Said to have appeared out of almost nowhere, this God of Science & Math (Tehuti) gave Humanity this 'Book of Life' as a means of instruction because it supposedly held all insights of The Creator and Creation. During Medieval Times, this text was viewed as an Alchemy Manual and Alchemists oftentimes hung a copy of it in their laboratories. They viewed it's hermetic contents as the 'black elixir' necessary to turn baser metals into gold. From a metaphysical perspective, this 'black elixir' was said to transmute the baseness of Man into the higher image and likeness of the true and living God.

Now, as a Creative Artist, I've always ceen Art as a symbolic 'black elixir' when it functions in a way to elevate (transmute) the condition and consciousness of People. I am conveying this idea with this Project. All of the Tracks on this Project were produced and recorded by me during different times of my life, different seasons and at different hours of the day. Actually there are even some Tracks like #13 (Doctor Waters) and #17 (Enterspace Nine) that I would recommend People experiment listening to through headphones, on repeat, while they go to sleep. Each track speaks a multitude of pages in my 'Book of Life' and will give my listeners an opportunity to experience part of an intimate/sacred Soundtrack to my life. Additionally, many People weren't aware that I produce/record Music so I also wanted to allow them an opportunity to experience this dimension of me. I call "The Emerald Tablet" 'The Mysticism of Sound and Music' and that's exactly what it is.

What Genre is "The Emerald Tablet"?

I consider any Music I produce/record as World Music and I always define it as a Soundtrack. Because Music is a universal language, I don't limit this expression. When you listen to the Soundtrack you'll hear influences from all over the World; from Irish Folk Music, HipHop, Classical Indian, Japanese and 1960's Soul Music. Sometimes I'm inspired to do a Poetry piece, other times I'll Rap. Other times I'll do what can be considered Spoken Word and sometimes I won't say anything at all. As far as the "Soundtrack" label is concerned, it's background Music to the life I've lived or presently live. By defining it as such I want People to understand that sound a part of the colorful backdrop of our lives. All of us have certain "Theme Music" that when we hear it we're teleported right back to that space and time when that sound made the deepest impression on us! It may be a Love Song, it may be a Party Song, it may be a Song that symbolizes a difficult time in our life. Whatever that visual impression it may be, this arrangement of sound (Music) conjures up images of page from our own 'Book of Life'. So, even if I did want to define it as a specific "Genre" I wouldn't even know what to call it! Lol It's Music.

What is the Track "Could It Be We" about?

"<u>Could It Be We</u>" was a Song I wrote that was inspired by a Queen whom I met some years back. Although upon first glance I felt a deep connection to her beyond words, which wasn't sexual, we went on to develop a relationship. My first line, *"Wisdom Equality all being born to Be Universally In Love's Destination"* summarizes that relationship. It's an acronym using Supreme Mathematics to spell "**WE BUILD**", and from that premise we went on to share many experiences together. This was a point in my life where I truly learned the most about the intimate and sensual dimensions of Love. At one point in this Song I say *"...and now it's intense/hearts throb like ancestral drums/that beat from the floor of the Atlantic/it's deep/discreet/divine/refined/giving sight to the blind/my Mind was in a timeless place/void of space where the heaven's be/I thought/Could It Be We"*. This was one of the ways I strived to describe the depths of what I thought and felt about the bond we created. One of the most significant parts of this relationship is how Time simply stood still when we were together. The World itself became peripheral and every challenge, trial and problem that we encountered from this vantage point, was approached with an unshakable sense of confidence, security and optimism. This is without question what the "We" represents in the title of this Song. The "Could It Be" is the worldly doubt and insecurity that can creep in whenever vessels of this magnitude become separated on a physical plane. In other words, Love transcends the physical veils that separate us; it's a journey of reunification with the essential source that bonds us. Sometimes I think People find themselves in dimensions of Love like this and it's a frightful place to be in. There were times we literally experienced a level of fusion; junctures where we truly became one being, not two separate selves striving to learn about or be as one. It reminds me of the lyrics Minnie Riperton said in her Song 'Inside My Love', "Two strangers/not strangers/only lacking the knowing/So willing/feeling/infinite growing". This sense of intuitive oneness, and the process of learning effective ways to sustain this state of existence, is what you'll feel and hear in this Track.

What is "Gods In Plain Clothes" about?

This Track showcases not only my lyricism b.u.t. also the intention of my lyrics as a vehicle of my way of life. The first verse is about my cultural credentials and I start off by saying, "*I know how deep the rabbit hole goes*". This is to let People know that gaining KOS (Knowledge of Self) and being on this journey of Self Realization is like being in Wonder Land. Not the type of hallucinogenic Wonderland 'Alice' was in, b.u.t. a Land of "Wonder" because now we're in a place where critically examining what we've been taught and are now learning typifies this uncharted terrain. In my second verse I describe an experience of someone who claims they want KOS who came amongst me. I talk about their disposition, what I assessed about them and how I responded to their approach. It's definitely important insight for anyone who has or is striving to educate someone. Also, when People hear about The NGE (The Nation of Gods and Earths) and particularly "The Gods", they either have this image in their Minds of Clash of the Titans or Characters from the TV Show Heroes with mythical powers when they think about who we are. Lol With "Gods In Plain Clothes", I wanted to give People a more realistic image of what our Culture is practically about.

When did your Musical Career start?

Even though I come from a Family with a Musical Background, I never actually learned to play any particular instrument proficiently. I've always had a profound love for Music and my first public Performance was in front of a couple hundred People at the tender age of 12. My Name was "Chilly C"; a beat-box prodigy for my older sister MC "Double K" while we performed in the Talent Show at our Annual Black Experience. I still remember the crowd and glaring lights. My Grand Ole Earth and my Old Earth played Piano. When my Ole Dad was in Junior High he was the Bass Player in a Band called "The El Morocco's". He also loved Jazz, Jimmy McGriff in particular, that ole Hammond B3 Organ, and collected a lot of Albums; which I took with me when I went away to College. So I've been around these elements of Culture all my Life and it was only natural that I would grow to develop a means of exploring and expressing these elements. Unbeknownst to me at the time, my journey into Music production/recording began in 1985; I was 10 years old scratching Albums on a dusty record player and using a radio and a tape recorder to loop breaks in beats on 60 minute Maxwell tapes. When HipHop first hit me I was electrified!! The Music, the Art, the Dance and the Cultural Expression itself moved me in a way that Instruments and no other music Genre could!! This Era is called 'The Golden Age' for a reason. Through the years I've always maintained an intimate relationship with HipHop. The Albums I collected, the Rhymes I recited and the Rhythms I hummed painted a colorful musical backdrop on a canvass called my childhood. Fast forward to the early 90's and I decided I wanted to start producing/recording Music. I was already writing/reading Poetry (prior to the Spoken Word Genre), writing Rhymes and performing my work at Coffee Houses, so now I wanted to get involved in the Music. I had no formal training, never even touched production equipment before and began to do research on what I needed in order to express the Music I was hearing in my head. One of the first things I did was purchase Magazines with equipment in it. Once I had my Mind set on what I wanted to get I cut some of the pictures out and taped them on my bedroom Wall. Even though I didn't have the money for this expensive equipment and was working as a Door to Door Salesman at the time, I had a "Determined Idea" and knew that I would get it one day. The reason I posted these pictures on my Wall was to program my Subconscious Mind; I would cee these images every morning I woke up, whenever I went into my room and before I went to bed at night. So along with Creative Visualization, Research, Hard Work and taking advantage of the doors (opportunities) that opened up for me production/recording wise, I was able to successfully do what I set out to do.

Who are your greatest Musical inspirations and why?
Wow! I have some many! Lol First and foremost I gotta give a shout out to my Enlightener's Enlightener 'Life Justice' who has helped broaden my scope and appreciation for Music in a way that's unimaginable! He's hipped me to Bob Dylan, who is in fact one of my favorite Writers, and various other Artists and Genres that I never even considered or even thought about. During his College Years he did a Radio Show called 'Wings of Expansion' that featured various types of Music. I've never met anyone with

such eclectic tastes and he's definitely made a huge impression on me. As far as lyricism is concerned, hands down The GZA. I love the precision and technical nature in which he constructs his lyrics where every word is emphatic. I love the visual imagery of Ghostface. I love the wit and effortlessness of Jay Z. I love the heart/passion of Tupac and I love the honesty/humility of the new Artist Stalley. Music Production wise I've been inspired by Artists like Isaac Hayes, Barry White, 4th Disciple, George Duke, Pete Rock, Roy Ayers, The RZA, Jagjit & Chitra Singh, Tru Master, Ultimate Spinach, DJ Premier, Quincy Jones, The Large Professor, Sly and The Family Stone and Fela Kuti to name a few.

How is the Album sales?

They're excellent! I didn't really expect the type of support I've been getting thus far from the little bit of Promotion I've done and I'm really appreciate that! People that aren't really into Music sometimes have a skewed view of putting an Album out though, especially if they're only aware of Top 40 Music. Some of the responses I've gotten from People is that it kinda conflicts with their preconceived ideas when they cee an actual Album you've created. Many People think you need a Major Record Company, a Commercial on TV and to be on '104 and Park' in order to have a legitimate Album you can purchase through legitimate Stores around the World. Lol To them, if you have a brunt copy of a CD with a name written on it in black marker that's more visually in sync with what they expect to cee. Although I do not have the Distribution that a Major Record Label has, anyone anywhere in the World can still order my Soundtrack at any Store you can purchase Music. I'm essentially selling Music out of my digital trunk. Another misconception that People have is that because you put out an Album your goal and intention is to go Platinum. I'm sure that is some People's actual intention, in the same way that some Writers are writing to win a Pulitzer Prize. Some People are also creating for the sole purpose of making money. Well I'm not and have never been that type of Creative Artist/Writer. Although these are talents I was naturally born with and have developed with hard word and help along the way, my greater purpose is to create a Legacy for Cultural Sustainability. In other words, I do what I do in order to make my personal contribution to Civilization and to help make this World a better place for the generations to follow. This is why with all the things that I do you never cee me constantly pushing People to financially support what I do. I produce it and there comes a time/opportunity where I think People will be able to benefit from what was produced, even when I'm no longer here! Those who are seeking it will ultimately find it, even if it's 5 years from now and I'm comfortable with that. For those who are and have been supportive of the things I do, I appreciate it very much, and I think one of best ways to show my appreciation is to continue being a resource/asset to help elevate (transmute) the condition and consciousness of People.

What's next?

Well I recently invested in another microphone so I've definitely been doing some production/recording. As far as what's next, I personally don't talk much about what I'm going to do, hope to do, want to do, might do and I'm dreaming about doing. I've found out that exposing premature ideas to the public is like exposing a newborn baby to the elements. I mean, even with "The Emerald Tablet" Soundtrack, no one had a clue about it; I just put it out! Over the years I've learned to operate in this way and I've been able to accomplish many long and short term goals by not talking about it b.u.t. being about it. I will say this, with the type of life I lead I'm always doing something and there's never a dull or boring moment. So you can expect to cee various other Projects in the future that I'm directly/indirectly involved in making manifest.

Effective Communication (TRC)

Whatever conflict we have with a person, lying beneath that discussion is always a Trust, Respect and Confidence (TRC) issue. If someone is late picking you up from somewhere an argument may begin about "being late" b.u.t. the underlying issue, because of their actions, you question how Trustworthy they are, how much Respect they have for your time and how much Confidence you can have in them to be pick you up the next time. Granted there may be legitimate reasons why they were late, yet this situation still diminishes the level of Trust, Respect and Confidence between you; especially if this is a habitual thing. Suppose you don't do the dishes or clean something up around the house. You and your Companion may get into an argument about "the dishes" or "cleaning up", yet the underlying issue is how your actions, or lack thereof, has made them question how Trustworthy you are as a Partner, how much Respect you have for the Home you share, and how much Confidence they have in you helping out.

The 21st Letter in our Supreme Alphabet is "U" and this is symbolic to 'You' or 'Universe'. Universe is also U-NI-Verse, You and I Verse or "You and I converse (communicate)". In other words, this tells us about the importance of Communication and Interrelationships. Communication is the ability to transfer/receive verbal and nonverbal data between People. Within a Culture, the vehicle we use to Communicate is language and body language. The Universe is everything, and everything is Interrelated (connected). Therefore, everything is always communicating, transferring/receiving Data in order to maintain an endless Circle of Life/Death. If is hasn't been communicated to us that it's -10° outside and we send our child out with shorts on, what will be the consequences? Suppose we saw a wild animal in our backyard and approached it -b.u.t. the dangers of rabies was never communicated to us? What can happen when the spoilage date on some food isn't communicated on its packaging? Imagine you got up super early and rushed to get to Class only to get there and find out it was rescheduled it; you didn't get the email... If Communication is important in these situations, imagine how important Communication is our most intimate bonds; Relationships.

Whenever we find ourselves in a conflict with one another, in a disagreement or a heated debate, find out what Trust, Respect and Confidence issues we are trying to Communicate. It's not about "the car" someone didn't put gas in they were allowed to use, it's a Trust, Respect and Confidence issue of how they handled the situation, regardless what the object was. Let's talk about how the handling of a situation has lessened the Trust, Respect and Confidence we have between eachother and what we need to do in order to restore/increase that Trust, Respect and Confidence! If we are not approaching conflicts, a disagreement or a heated debate from the perspective of You and I Verse or "You and I converse (communicate)", we will find ourselves expressing 'You and I "vs/versus"', where it becomes a battle to prove who deserves the most Trust, Respect and Confidence. An example of this would be an argument starting about "the dishes" going into somebody getting off at 5pm and not coming home until 6:30pm, the Event the other person missed last Spring, the female who's always smiling up in your face at work, to her single girlfriends you don't like... ALL of this goes back to Trust, Respect and Confidence issues that are a fine mist our naked eye can hardly detect. By approaching our conflicts in this matter, it then becomes a question of how legitimate or illegitimate these Trust, Respect and Confidence issues are. Sometimes a person honestly didn't know or they may be culturally insensitive. This is alot more productive than arguing with someone about leaving one sock in the dryer or why you didn't return somebody's phone call. We may find out that it's not legitimate and they/we have Trust, Respect and Confidence issues "regardless to whom or what." Communicate!

I once experienced a situation where a person made a selfish decision where I questioned how much I could Trust them, the level of Respect they had for others and my Confidence in them to do the right thing in the future. The irony is that when I was in the same situation before them, I chose to make decisions that they could Trust, Respect and have Confidence in, so I had more Trust, Respect and Confidence in them to reciprocate the care/consideration. We briefly talked about the surface issue yet never addressed the Trust, Respect and Confidence issues that were created based upon how they chose to handle the situation. Maybe if I would have better communicated (21: You and I verse/converse) that it wasn't about "the car" itself, b.u.t. how they chose to handle the situation about the car, we could have come to a better Understanding (3). 21 being the inverse of the 12th Letter (L; Love), maybe this would have given them an opportunity to be more introspective about how Trust, Respect and Confidence are elements of Love we claimed to have for one another. Maybe if I would have used the actual words 'Trust', 'Respect' and 'Confidence' to describe how their personal actions diminished our Bond, they would have ceen (3) what I was saying and we could have resolved the conflict and disagreement that turned into a heated debate. I use the word "maybe" because sometimes you can tell a person about how their actions diminished the level of Trust, Respect and Confidence between you and they simply can't cee it. Sometimes we can't cee it when someone tells us that. It's possible that they/we can be that Hedonistic or Narcissistic where they/we have a difficult time forming real bonds of Trust, Respect and Confidence with others. If they/we are changing social circles like musical chairs every few years, they/we can never seem to maintain a Relationship for more than a few years, and it's ALWAYS someone else's fault why they/we no longer talk to People, this is probably the case...

In conclusion, when I was a child my Parents always coordinated Family Meetings and "Communication" was a buzzword in my household. This is what kept us close, strengthened our bonds and gave us an opportunity to learn how to Trust, Respect and have Confidence in one another. We learned how to get past surface issues and discuss what we've done or what was done to us to diminish the level of Trust, Respect and Confidence we had for one another. Most importantly, we learned about what we needed to do in order to restore/increase that Trust, Respect and Confidence! I appreciate my Parents for having the wisdom/foresight to provide me and my siblings with these tools. In any Bond, the highest Value lies within that Relationship, so the willingness/ability to communicate (Word) our Trust, Respect and Confidence issues is an important part of securing that Bond, especially when these are Relationships for Life. Effective

Communication is what makes these Relationships not only possible b.u.t. also enduring. On the flip side, Effective Communication also allows you to cee if People are willing/able to be invested in an enduring Relationship. Because it's impossible to Value a Bond where the actions of one or both People continually diminish the Trust, Respect and Confidence in that Relationship... until there is no, thing, left...

Historiography

The Science of History

When you ask the average person about History, they'll ramble off some dates that describe events as "something that happened in the past". Even though this is a very linear way of looking at History, most People still fail to connect the dots of how these past events helped shape the present and potentially the future.

Take a brief moment to look around you... If there's food around you that's History because it was made in the past, willfully a short time ago. Even if it's fresh, it either grew in the past or it's ingredients came from the past. There are hundreds of children who die from food poisoning each year because someone neglected to read the spoilage date on a food item... Every thing you're wearing right now was made in the past. Even if you sewed it today, the materials were made in the past. The device you're using to read this Article, all of the objects around you, the Building you're in right now or Building's you cee around you were all made in the past. Even the Plants and Animals; they too grew from the past. In School we were taught that History is a separate subject. The reality is, all subjects, and their methodologies, are Historical. If it's Math, its Arabic Numerals and methods were made in the past. Science? All of their definitions, processes, discoveries, and observations were made in the past. Even Physical Education (Gym) is History because somebody came up with jumping jacks! So you cee, History is not dates about past events, History is a present day reality wherever we go and there is no way around it. History (the past) is in, on and around us. As a matter of fact, what you are reading at this very moment is a past event!

"Historiography" is the critical examination of past events for the purpose of accurately writing History. Historiography is a forensic approach towards the writing of History, not the glossed over stuff we've been taught since Elementary School. The reason there's even a word called "Historiography" is because People understood the importance (value) of recognizing how events of the past shape and mode the present and ultimately our future. More importantly, People realized how 'Psychohistory' predetermined History. The structures that were built in the past, which is every building you cee around you, were designed according to specific dimensions (length, width, and depth). Because you are inside of these structures you are subject to conform to these dimensions. If there's a stairwell you simply have to utilize it to get upstairs, if there's not a door there you can't walk through the wall, and etc.. If we no longer want to conform to these dimensions then we can modify this structure to suit our needs; yet we still have to conform to the rules, regulations, and building materials (from the past) that we will be using to modify this structure. Another option is building from the ground up and making our own structures! Well keep in Mind that any past event is a structure just the same. These intangible events are structures composed of ideas, inventions, experiences and attitudes that produce the Psychological and Socioeconomic dimensions of today. And like a building, we too are subject to conform to these ideas, inventions, experiences and attitudes that determine the dimensions of today and potentially our future. So our very existence depends upon our ability to process/interpret how these past events, that are in, on and around us, affect our lives today and can possibly shape our future.

In a Society of tangible and intangible structures that were made in the past, we must ask ourselves, "How do they shape the Psychological and Socioeconomic dimensions of today?" As I've said, these 'tangible' (buildings, materials, and objects) and 'intangible' structures (ideas, inventions, experiences and attitudes) are in, on and around us! Those who don't care to critically examine these past events (structures) are ill equipped to psychologically and socioeconomically process/interpret the present reality we exist in. In other words, if you don't know where something came from, it's impossible to know where it's at, where it should be, or where it's potentially going! Suppose that 'thing' you don't know about is your Self... Wherever you cee People who lack a sense of Historiography, who possess a topical idea of History, you'll cee a People who are vulnerable and "easily led." The Occupy Wallstreet Movement that's going on at this present moment reflects a great majority of this segment of our population, and it's a beautiful thing ceeing People critically examining where things came from, are, and can go!

One thing I've realized for a while now and more recently in everyday conversations or even FB discussions People, is that they don't Mind discussing how Jimi Hendrix shaped/molded the present day reality of Rock Music, how The Fab Five Freshman changed the uniform landscape of Basketball, or how NOW (National Organization for Women) helped modify the gender roles of Women in America today. Yet when it comes to those past events that happened over a period of generations like The Genocide of Native Americans, The Trans-Atlantic Slave Trade, Chattel Slavery, Segregation, Institutional Sexism/Racism, Colonialism, and etc.. People, Black & White alike, start acting strange... Instead of actively engaging in a process of critically examining these past events, like they're clearly doing everything else, they either avoid it, deny it, run from it, hide from it, or even attack you for bringing these things up. It's like while everything else is valid, they don't even want to consider how the 'tangible' (buildings, materials, and objects) and 'intangible' structures (ideas, inventions, experiences and attitudes) made from "these" past events determine the Psychological and Socioeconomic dimensions of the today and potentially our future. The fact that "these" past events usually didn't even happen to the People (Caucasians) who don't want to even think about it tells you something in it of itself... It also tells you a lot about their level of consideration, respect, and ultimately love for those People (Black/Non-White) who's

Ancestors directly experienced these past events. Again, if you don't consider where something came from, it's impossible to consider where it's at, how you should treat it, or where it's potentially going. Does that make sense?

Now how can we began to look at History as Historiography? One of the obvious things to consider about being willing/able to critically examine History is that People have to be studious, courageous, and honest about what they're discovering. Oftentimes, many of the 'tangible' (buildings, materials, and objects) and 'intangible' structures (ideas, inventions, experiences and attitudes) we come across are hurtful, painful, shameful, and etc.., yet we must be willing/able to accept these things as a valid location on the map of Human Geography. A Map that gives us greater insight into many of the Psychological and Socioeconomic dimensions we may/may not conform to today. This is why it's important to engage ourselves in this process, because our Families and our Communities will undoubtedly benefit from this insight. I am a living example of this and I can't thank my Parents enough for educating me and my siblings about how past events not only help shape our present day realities, b.u.t. how this insight empowers us to change/modify these past structures or build new one's to meet the needs of a brighter future for our Family, Communities, People, and Humanity.

In closing, I want to address those of us who have this "Island-like" Philosophy when it comes to ourselves and our Relationships. The belief, feelings, or ideas that the problems going on with "other" People, in "other" Families, and in "other" Communities has nothing to do with you is a very selfish, uneducated, flawed lens to view the World through. First of all, you do not stand alone because you most likely didn't even produce the toilet paper you used today. Even if you actually did, there are many People who made a collective contribution so that product (toilet paper) could become a reality. Even our very physical existence hinged upon the contributions of a Mother and Father, so it's impossible to get around the fact that we are all here because of others; directly and indirectly. Now think about the illogic in such Philosophies like, "I don't care what anybody thinks", "I'm doing me", and "This is MY relationship and I don't care what anybody says", etc... Think about how selfish this thought process is when these Individuals and Relationships are being FULLY SUPPORTED by the contributions of past events and sacrifices of others; 'tangible' (buildings, materials, and objects) and 'intangible' structures (ideas, inventions, experiences and attitudes). To live a life where we are consistently receiving from others..., yet we are not sharing/giving in return or may even care less about what others feel/think is absolutely unacceptable. Imagine how long we'd live if everybody else embraced that same Philosophy...

Imagine where we would be if everybody said, "The problems going on with 'other' People, in 'other' Families and in 'other' Communities has nothing to do with me"... The bottom line is this: The Universe (everything) is Interdependent and one of the keys to obtaining true Peace, Harmony, Equality, and Sustainability is our willingness/ability to recognize that we are all connected and rely upon the alternating currents of all of us giving/receiving in this World; regardless if we are in a Major City or a Remote Village. So any Individual or Relationship that holds fast to Philosophies like, "I don't care what anybody thinks", "I'm doing me", and "This is MY relationship and I don't care what anybody says", etc... have put themselves in a position to get blindsided by the Universe, because everything is Interdependent, including these Individuals and Relationships. When we are accurately examining History (Historiography), we are considering the Interdependence of TIME; the interrelationship between the past, the present and the future. Therefore, when we don't consider these interrelationships, it's only a matter of TIME before these Individuals and Relationships are forced to bear witness to this Interdependent reality; a reality check that always happens at a TIME we least expect it! So start engaging in some of these tough discussions about past events we've been selectively avoiding and in denial about. We cannot afford to be apathetic and/or ignorant to these things because these Attitudes/Perspectives will continue to produce serious consequences for our future generations. We need to learn from one another about ways WE can solve the present World's problems (Psychological, Socioeconomic, Political, Environmental, Educational, etc.) because they are clearly affecting 'us' all and potentially shaping 'our' future.

Love is Pain - Love Hurts

LOVE, like the word 'Spiritual', it's one of the broadest and most ambiguous terms we use. So People have many different ideas about what Love is and how it functions. People look for Relationships based upon these ideas, form Relationships based upon these ideas, and seek to maintain Relationships based upon these ideas. Regardless what our ideas are about Love, one of the most important questions we can ask ourselves is, "Is my idea of Love a sustainable model for Relationships?" In otherwords, "Is my definition of Love built to last?"

Imagine if my Philosophy of Love was, "Love is Pain" or "Love Hurts". Since such a Philosophy charts the course of my Life, this means is that in all of my Relationships I approach them seeking and anticipating some painful experience or the opportunity to get hurt. Why would I do this? Because according to my Philosophy, pain/hurt equals Love. This also means that if I'm not experiencing any pain/hurt in a Relationship, it must not be Love. A person who embraces this Philosophy tends to self sabotage good, stable, productive Relationships because it contradicts their Philosophy of Love. So instead of accepting the reality that their Philosophy is wrong, they'd rather destroy the Relationship to make their Philosophy "look" right... Another name for this Philosophy is Masochism, and many of our People who embrace it don't even realize that the reason their Relationships don't, won't, and can't last is because of this Philosophy. Again, we must ask ourselves, "Is my idea of Love a sustainable model for Relationships?"

There are basically two types of People who embrace this Philosophy:

1.) People who think/believe "Love is Pain" or "Love Hurts", yet they still try to get into Relationships with others.

2.) People who think/believe "Love is Pain" or "Love Hurts", and they shun Relationships with others because they don't want to feel pain or be hurt.

Both of these People developed this Philosophy from personally going through or observing mental, emotional, financial, and/or physical abusive situations, and thus concluded that abuse (pain/hurt) comes along with the territory and validates Love. The fact that we, as Adults, can cee the obvious illogic and flaws in this Philosophy is an obvious indication that this person experienced/observed and came to this conclusion at very early part of their development: Only someone who's lacking the cognitive, intellectual, and emotional maturity/ability to cee how illogical and flawed this Philosophy is would come to this kind of conclusion; a child. More often than not, they quietly made this conclusion so long ago that they don't even recall when they made it –especially if there was severe trauma associated with experiencing/observing that abuse. From that point onward, their lives primarily consist of a series of abusive/self sabotaged Relationships or avoidance of Relationships altogether, as a means to find evidence to support this conclusion they already have: "Love is Pain" or "Love Hurts". The only thing sustainable about a "Love is Pain" or "Love Hurts" Philosophy is the mental, emotional, financial, and/or physical abuse that a person seeks/anticipates. The only thing sustainable about being in a Relationship with someone who has a "Love is Pain" or "Love Hurts" Philosophy is the mental, emotional, financial, and/or physical abuse you will receive from them, or the mental, emotional, financial, and/or physical abuse you'll be provoked to give them.

Within The Five Percenters, "Love is Pain" or "Love Hurts" is obviously not a Philosophy we embrace. It is a complete contradiction to our Perspective of Love, and how Love functions to sustain model Relationships. Through our Cultural Curriculum, here are a few basic points we know and teach about Love:

L: 12th Letter in the Alphabet

First and foremost, the letter 'L' is a 90° angle; a Right Angle. There is nothing fundamentally right about Love resulting in pain/hurt. That's equivalent to saying that mental, emotional, financial, and/or physical abuse is right... Since the #12 is comprised of Knowledge (1) and Wisdom (2), it takes a level of Awareness and Discernment (cognitive, intellectual, and emotional maturity/ability) to recognize that abuse is not Love. Initially, this is their greatest challenge because they haven't grown to Understand (3) the illogic/flaw in a "Love is Pain" or "Love Hurts" Philosophy. Just like anyone who 'commits' and/or 'accepts' abuse in a Relationship, their greatest challenge is recognizing that this is not Love!

The letter 'L' also represents the Principle called 'Love Hell or Right', and this is exactly the stance we take upon coming in contact with People who embrace a "Love is Pain" or "Love Hurts" Philosophy; you can either Love Hell (pain/hurt), or Love Right. It's meant to acknowledge the pain/hurt People may experience in Relationships yet it denies pain/hurt as an integral component or result of what Love ultimately is. A common phrase you'll hear Gods/Earths express is, "Love is the highest degree of Understanding", and it's impossible to understand something, especially Love, when you're in pain or hurt. If you ever had a toothache, cramps, an earache, death in the family, etc., you 'understand' exactly what I mean...

Some Five Percenters have a misconception that 'Love Hell or Right' means one must accept Hell (pain/hurt) as a part of Love, in order for it to be Right. This is untrue and is more of reflection of a "Love is Pain" or "Love Hurts" Philosophy that they grafted onto our Cultural Worldview. What 'Love Hell or Right' does mean is that we must be Aware (1) and Discerning (2) enough to avoid these kinds of Philosophies that entertain the idea that pain/hurt (abuse) is somehow intrinsic to Love. It also means that in Love, we must be willing/able to 'go through' any trials and tribulations (Hell) in order to adhere to what's ultimately Right ("Just and True" 37/1-40). If we aren't willing/able to avoid these Philosophies and endure trials and tribulations, our Relationships can't/won't be Right because we will, without a doubt, experience the same Hellish results as those who embrace these illogical/flawed Philosophies. The Principle of 'Love Hell or Right' charges a person with the responsibility of gaining the highest degree of Understanding from any/all experiences, in order to rise above any/all experiences to do what's ultimately Right ("Just and True" 37/1-40). A person who thinks/believes that "Love is Pain" or "Love Hurts" is not thinking about the responsibility of Understanding or rising above anything, because according to their Philosophy, Love is equivalent to, not transcendent of, the pain/hurt they may 'feel'. To them, pain/hurt is as far as Love goes...

At this point it is very important to understand that when one person subscribes to the Principle of 'Love Hell or Right' and another person embraces the Philosophy that "Love is Pain" or "Love Hurts", it's impossible for that Relationship to work. While one person will always be striving to gain an Understanding and rise above any/all experiences to do what's ultimately Right, the other person will be seeking, anticipating, accepting, AND oftentimes manufacturing painful/hurtful experiences -because in their Mind, "If It Ain't Rough It Ain't Right". These are two entirely different Perspectives that can't be reconciled, and a Relationship like this will not work out. Some of us are under the illusion that we can win a person over who has a "Love is Pain" or "Love Hurts" Philosophy. So we get into a Relationship or even marry them and work overtime trying to prove their Philosophy wrong. It never occurs to us that any pain/hurt they 'feel', whether true or imagined, our fault or not, will only serve to validate their Philosophy. It also never occurs to us that it's impossible to avoid 'feelings' in a Relationship, which ultimately means, something will always end up being wrong (painful/hurtful). Why? Because a person who thinks/believes "Love is Pain" or "Love Hurts" comes into a Relationship looking for what's wrong with it. So what begins as our noble quest to show & prove or even save a person from themselves quickly turns into a life (or lifetime) of perpetual setbacks, misery, and disappointments; similar to a hamster running around in a maze that ALWAYS leads to nowhere... Although those of us who at least have Supreme Mathematics and the Supreme Alphabet have the tools to avoid this dilemma, many of us fail to apply the Principle of 'Love Hell or Right' for various reasons. As I stated, deep down inside some of us may really agree with a "Love is Pain" or "Love Hurts" Philosophy so we accept the abuse. Some of us may really believe that we can change someone, so instead of recognizing their Philosophy "cannot be reformed" (34/1-40), we "give all we have and all within our power" in hopes that one day they'll cee the light (40/1-40). Giving all we have and all within our power is not wrong in it of itself, it's just the wrong approach/procedure in this situation because you're trying to give something to someone who clearly doesn't want it. As a matter of fact, the consequential pain/hurt you'll 'feel' from their rejection of what you strive to give them only serves the purpose of further validating their Philosophy that "Love is Pain" or "Love Hurts"...

Justice Jewel (10th) is Love

In our 12 Jewels the 10th Jewel or 'Justice Jewel' is Love. When most People consider Justice that don't consider its Relationship to Love. This tells you a lot about how they view

Relationships as a whole... Justice being more than rewards and penalties based upon one's ways & actions. Justice, in part, represents Integrity (Justness), Fairness, Harmony, and Equilibrium (Equality). These are all components of Love, and there is no Integrity (Justness), Fairness, Harmony, and Equilibrium (Equality) in a "Love is Pain" or "Love Hurts" Philosophy. In order to successfully demonstrate these components, one must be considerate, caring, respectful, honorable, committed, affectionate, sincere, and a host of other qualities in order to reinforce a sense of Justice. Can you imagine going before a Judge who doesn't possess the components of Justice or the qualities that reinforce it? Do you think you'll get a fair shake? Well imagine the results of a Relationship with someone who doesn't possess the components of Justice or the qualities that reinforce it... It's impossible for a Relationship like this to be Loving and offer someone a fair shake.

Since the Justice Jewel "Love" is '10' or Knowledge (1) Cipher (0), Love is Knowing the importance of the Cipher; Reciprocity. A Relationship is a Cipher, a Bond. In order to maintain that Bond, the components of Justice (Integrity [Justness], Fairness, Harmony, and Equilibrium [Equality]) and the qualities that reinforce it (considerate, caring, respectful, honorable, committed, affectionate, sincere, and etc.) are held together through Reciprocity. Reciprocity is the willingness/ability to complement eachother through mutual, corresponding, interdependent exchanges and interactions that sustain this Bond. To reciprocate is a process that begins with sharing/giving, not taking! It's interesting to note that when many People are asked about Love and Relationships, they usually begin by talking about what they want or desire to get from somebody. RARELY do you hear someone begin a conversation about Love and Relationships talking about what they're willing/able to actually give... It tells you a lot about their ideas concerning Reciprocity, and if they ever even thought about it at all, now doesn't it? Also, think about what kind of Reciprocity a "Love is Pain" or "Love Hurts" Philosophy demonstrates. Would you like to be on the receiving end of that?

Justice functions as a System of checks & balances designed to maintain stability. Therefore, Justice is "Just I Cee Equality". In a Bond (Relationship), it's Just "Us", not you and me, "Us". This is important to understand because some People may assume that the 'I' in Just I Cee Equality is an individual or 'I' as in EGO. When it's about "Us", not you and me, "We" approach a Relationship realizing that "Our" Bond hinges upon the components of Justice (Integrity [Justness], Fairness, Harmony, and Equilibrium [Equality]) and the qualities that reinforce it (considerate, caring, respectful, honorable, committed, affectionate, sincere, and etc.). In otherwords, we are essentially

One (1) and that's how our Cipher (0) must function in order to keep it together!

In conclusion, these are just "a few" of the many examples, illustrations, and break-downs we learn about Love within our Cultural Curriculum, and I didn't even go through the many examples, illustrations, and break-downs within 120 Lessons. The point in sharing this was to demonstrate how our Culture possesses various Cultural references that fully explore, expound upon, and define Love, its components/qualities, and how it does/doesn't function. And as we explore, expound upon, and define Love, we examine what adds up and what doesn't. We consider the validity of such statements like, "Love is Love", "Love knows no Color", "Love is how I feel", "I fell in Love", "I Love you but I'm not in Love with you", "Love is Pain", "Love Hurts", and of course any other ideas we hear about Love. Make no mistake about it, that it's a very sick, abnormal, Masochistic Psychology that embraces the Philosophy that "Love is Pain" or "Love Hurts". Love does not consist of nor is it equivalent to mental, emotional, financial, and/or physical abuse. A person who thinks/believes this is only capable of hurting themselves and causing pain to others. Until they've actually critically analyzed the illogic/flaws in such a Philosophy, to cee why it hasn't/doesn't work to sustain Relationships, they will continue to hurt themselves and cause pain to others. This doesn't mean

120

that People like this are somehow diabolical or deliberately out to hurt themselves and cause pain to others. They may be nice, attractive, funny, social, and even high functioning intellectuals who simply embrace a Philosophy about Love, and probably other Philosophies about Life, that ultimately hurts them and causes pain to others. They simply haven't learned how to Love someone or sustain a Relationship... Keep in Mind that they may have been embracing this Philosophy for the last 25 years, so building with them, investing time with them, talking to them, praying with them, and etc. is not enough to change almost a whole generation of illogical/flawed thinking. This is the reality of what you're dealing with, not what you hope things to one day be. In our 10/1-40 we learn that "we lost no more time searching for that-that does not exist" in regards to a Mystery God. Well the same thing applies to searching for something that someone doesn't and cannot cee in themselves. If they ultimately do, it must be under their own power and "in their own 'GOOD' time" (39/1-40) because "Self" is the only "Savior" ('S' is the 19th Letter in the Supreme Alphabet). It's our job to make Knowledge Born about the Principle of 'Love Hell or Right', not try to make them, force them, or coerce them to think/believe anything differently, ESPECIALLY someone who, based upon their Philosophy, is fighting against your Love from the door! I know many of us believe that nobody's hopeless, and I agree. Yet there are People who think/believe they're hopeless based upon the illogical/flawed Philosophies they embrace. Because of their allegiance to these ideas, they become incorrigible and there's nothing you can do about it mentally, emotionally, financially and/or physically. There is a lot of "Self" work a person has to do before they're even willing, let alone capable of, Understanding that "Love IS NOT Pain" or "Love DOES NOT Hurt". It takes a lot of sacrifice, studiousness and commitment on their part, and up until this point in their Life, you may be the first person who ever showed them anything different. The reality is that once a person has reached their 30's and above holding fast to an illogical/flawed Philosophy like this, it's possible yet very rare that they are willing AND capable to make the sacrifice, be studious, and have the commitment to change their Philosophy on Life. If you think/believe otherwise, you're in for a World of pain/hurt, because that's what they ultimately believe Love is; pain/hurt. And until they actually think/believe anything different, that's all you can and will get from them.

Family Dynamics 101

"Study their Family Dynamics" was the response I received from my Ole Earth at the naïve age of 12 -when informing me about what I needed to think about when looking for a girlfriend. As some of you are already aware, she was a Psychologist with a Minor Degree in Sociology, so this type of language wasn't unfamiliar to my home environment. Phrases like 'Self Mutilation', 'Paranoid Schizophrenic', and medical conditions like 'Microcephalic', 'Anorexia Nervosa', etc. were all things I had a basic knowledge of in my pre-teens. When it came to girls, one of the most significant things my Ole Earth taught me, that took me many years to actually begin to understand, was the phrase, "Study their Family Dynamics". Because I was young, this of course was a very heavy concept to consider. My hormones were already kicking in and all I really cared about is if a girl was pretty or not. Interestingly enough, People my age today, and older, still choose Companions using that Philosophy: All I care about is if he/she looks good! Anyway, slowly over time, and through many trials, errors, and accomplishments, I finally began to get what she meant! Let me break it down...

Family Dynamics

It's obvious what our physical Family is comprised of: Father, Mother, maybe Siblings, Grandparents, and other kin. The word "Dynamic" is another name for 'Power, Force, Energy, and Influence.' A "Dynamic" is a 'Power, Force, Energy, and Influence' that motivates or moves something. In this case we're talking about the various elements within a Family that has had the 'Power, Force, Energy, and Influence' to motivate or move someone who's a Member of that Family. When we look at this 'Power, Force, Energy, and Influence' that motivates/moves People, we are referring to the Principles and Values they learned, or lack thereof, as a child growing up. Family introduces and exposes us to our first Lessons about Relationships. By learning about a person's upbringing, and the Relationships they had/have with their Family, we learn about some of the most significant influences that helped shape and mold this person into who they are or are not today. When we enter into any kind of Relationship with People be it platonic, business, or significant, we are having a Relationship with their Family's 'Power, Force, Energy, and Influence'. Even if this person has chosen to socially cut themselves off from their Family, we are still in a Relationship with their Family's 'Power, Force, Energy, and Influence' because their Family Members are still present within their DNA (genotype/phenotype) –which is something they will never escape, even though they may like to. This leads me to my point...

When we study the Dynamics or 'Power, Forces, Energy, and Influences' going on within a person's Family Relationships, we get a better idea of what their inclinations/potential may be if they established a Family Relationship with us. We first learn about the rightness/wrongness of Family and Relationships through the one we were born into. So our willingness/ability to work things out with the Family we were 'given' is a good indication of our potential willingness/ability to work things out with the Family we 'made' or want to 'get... This is very important to recognize because our Family is our First 'Training Unit' when it comes to Relationships. This is where we first learn about fairness, cheating, forgiveness, anger, disappointment, sadness, embarrassment, joy, and everything else imaginable when it comes to establishing, building, maintaining, and severing Relationships. How we handled/handle these challenges, with Family Members, who we will be connected to for the rest of our lives, informs others about our skills/tolerance to handle these challenges with others, who we are not obligated to be connected to for the rest of our lives. In other words, if I don't have the skills to handle my own brother's attitude, how am I qualified to handle a dude with the same attitude that isn't my brother, and has no 'Family' obligations/ties to me? If I lack the tolerance (endure/sustain) to deal with my own Mother's behavior, how will I be able to tolerate a female Companion who may demonstrate the same behavior, and has no 'Family' obligations/ties to me? If it's easy to walk away from meeting the challenges/demands our own Family presents us with, then it will be easier to walk away from People who aren't Family, when they present us with the same challenges/demands...

Studying a person's Family Dynamics means to examine how a person handled/handles their Family Relationships and what 'Power, Force, Energy, and Influence' (Principles and Values) is at play in those Relationships. If you're a male, examine how a female interacts with her Siblings (if she has any) and Parents, especially her Father. Is her Father nothing more than her ATM Machine? Does she talk to him like he is her peer? Does she make sure she introduces a guy she's interested in to her Father? Does she even know her Father and when she does mention him, does she refer to him as 'her sperm donor'? The 'Power, Force, Energy, and Influence' (Principles and Values) that define this Father/Daughter interaction, sets the potential stage for Principles and Values that are likely to express themselves in the male/female Relationships in her life. If a female doesn't have the skills/tolerance to deal with her own 'Father', what makes you think she'll have the skills/tolerance to deal with you as her Man -who she can easily walk away from? Her Father was the first Man in her life, whether he was there or not, and how she primarily thinks/feels about him being there or not, is very important for you to know. Why? You may one day become this Man; a Father, to the children she has for you, and her thoughts/feelings about you being there or not, has the potential of being passed on, entertained, and embraced by your children. The same Scenario goes for females who're studying the Family Dynamics of a potential male Companion. How does he talk and interact with his Mother? Does she control his life, and if so, how does he handle it? Does he curse her out when he doesn't get something he wants? Is his Mother still cleaning up the messes he makes? Does he speaking kindly and respectfully of/to his Mother? Again, the 'Power, Force, Energy, and Influence' (Principles and Values) that define this Mother/Son interaction sets the potential stage for Principles and Values that are likely to express themselves in the female/male Relationships in his life.

Keep in Mind that this isn't a death sentence on anyone who has Dysfunctional Family Relationships because we all do in some form or fashion. The question is, "What are we striving to do about resolving our thoughts, feelings, and dealings with these Dysfunctions?" This is an appeal to those of us who tend to overlook the importance of studying Family Dynamics; ours and those of a potential Companion. This is an appeal to those of us who believe we can develop the skills/tolerance (endurance) to handle these issues by simply trying to disconnect ourselves from People who we will be connected to for the rest of our life; Family. This does not mean that we have to sit around and agree with or accept everything our Family does, b.u.t. it does mean that we have to come to some resolution and develop some type of stratagem to handle the reality that we'll be connected to them for the rest of our lives, and the extended Family (children) that will be born into our Family. If a person doesn't have the willingness/ability to agree to disagree with their own Family, it's not likely they're going to have the willingness/ability to agree to disagree with someone else, an outsider, when presented with the same Perspective/Scenario. So instead of developing a resolution or stratagem, many of us simply cut People off, oftentimes for very petty issues, and it often takes serious or even tragic situations to make us realize this pettiness and bring us back together, even if it's just temporarily... It's this lack of resolution or stratagem that People bring with them into a potential Relationship; it's called baggage. We all have baggage, b.u.t. everyone doesn't carry it the same way, nor does everyone have the same intention and ability to do something about it.

In conclusion, I want to encourage all of us to keep in Mind that in all Relationships there is always a 'Dynamic' at play, and Family is the most fundamental 'Power, Force, Energy, and Influence' because we are born into it. This Dynamic, Family, is the first 'Power, Force, Energy, and Influence' that was instrumental in shaping our Principles, Values, and ultimately our Worldview. Even those things that we don't do, think, feel, or value any longer still represent a 'Power, Force, Energy, and Influence' in our life; they are at the root of our considerations of making change (i.e. "I'll never eat salisbury steak again because...", "I always choose a guy/girl that looks like that because..."). Our Family is our first Training Unit, whether we were being taught to lie or tell the truth. This is the hand we were dealt, and how we play this hand will tell a lot about our proclivities in playing with others -and how we even perceive the hand they were dealt in life -whether it's worst, the same, or better than ours. We first learn about the rightness and wrongness of Family and Relationships through the one we were born into. How we work things out with the Family we were 'given', is a good indication of our potential to work things out with the Family we 'made' or the Family we 'want' to make. If you want to judge a Man's degree of forgiveness, watch his willingness/ability to forgive his own Siblings/Parents. If you want to cee a Woman's ability to sacrifice, watch how and what she sacrifices for her child(ren), and how she thinks/feels about it. If you want to assess if a male has a basic level of respect for females, watch how he talks about, addresses, and treats the females in his Family. Likewise, if you want to assess if a female has a basic level of respect for males, watch how she talks about, addresses, and treats the males in her Family. If the way he/she chooses to talk about, address, and treat their own Family isn't good, I wouldn't have high hopes for them having the skills/tolerance (endurance) to build and maintain a good Family with me. Why? Because it's questionable where they will actually get the skills/tolerance (endurance) from; they obviously didn't develop them at home. Even though my Ole Earth said, "Study their Family Dynamics", I will go a step further in saying, "Study 'our' Family Dynamics". WE ALL BRING something to the table; some things we'd love to be remembered for, and some things we'd probably like to forget. Being aware, honest, and resolute about what WE ALL BRING will mean all the difference in World when it comes to the quality of our Relationships and the integrity of our Family Units.

Professionalism

and

Public Images of Civilization

'Consideration' is our ability to think about how our words/actions effect ourselves and others before we speak or act upon something. It's a process of making sure we do the Knowledge (Aware) before the Wisdom (Discernment), because we Understand (See) the effects of our words/actions. To Civilized People, this is a Righteous obligation, not an option or elective...

With the popularity of Reality Shows and 'rewarding bad behavior' approach towards the crass, uncivilized, and unprofessional attitudes displayed in mainstream HipHop, basic 'Consideration' has become a lost art amongst People. I can understand those who have an allegiance to these American Cultural Trends that are going with this flow, b.u.t. this mentality/behavior is totally unacceptable for Five Percenters or any person, whether Christian, Muslim, Buddhist, or etc.., who professes to live in accordance to a standard of Civilization, Righteousness, or Godliness.

Recently I had a conversation about the importance of being aware of what we say/do as a Representative/Contact Person within our Culture. Part of this conversation involved me sharing some of my experience as a Public Figure who's been doing Community Work for many years now. As an add-on to that conversation, I just wanted to share with you a few points of interest.

First and foremost, it's important to understand that whenever we take a stance of responsibility within our Families and Communities, we are expressing a position of Leadership. This is Leadership because we are actively involving ourselves in the solution process of addressing current/future problems. Leadership doesn't just mean you're THE Head, Leadership means you're a part of the 'ship' to 'lead' People in the right direction. Anytime we take responsibility for Leadership, we must be 'Considerate'; able to think about how our words/actions effect ourselves and others before we speak or act upon something. To claim responsibility and then minimize or dismiss the importance of maintaining a Professional, Mature, and Respectable Public Image to those within our Family and Community is not showing a sense of 'Consideration'. The People whom we are claiming to assist are already looking towards us for guidance and support in addressing their needs, and to have an Attitude like "it doesn't matter what People think", "What I do is my business", "I'm not a Leader", or anything else that displays no 'Consideration' for our constituents is detrimental to building positive/consistent Relationships with them. For example: It's like working with the youth during the day and then not caring if they cee you selling crack on the block at night... It's like talking about how much of a Five Percenter I am on social media one minute and then five minutes later posting about how the b*tches/n*ggas had it poppin at the strip club last night... Again, 'Consideration' is our ability to think about how our words/actions effect ourselves/others before we speak or act upon something. It's impossible to demonstrate and maintain effect Leadership without a level of 'Consideration'.

Secondly, in order to even be 'Considerate', we must be able to listen. That's right, LISTEN. Most People don't know how to listen and that's one of the main reasons why we don't learn anything –from others or through our life experiences. Non-listeners either cut People off so they can say whatever they want to say, or simply wait for People to take a breath so they can jump in and say whatever they want to say. Add unbridled emotions to this otherwise poor display of communication and it's a sure shot recipe for disaster. Rarely do you cee effective communication taking place between People where one person speaks while the other is listening, and then they exchange roles until they both have an understanding about the information being exchanged. It's a skill! A discipline even, and not everyone is interested in really hearing what others have to say. If you listen closely you'll notice that they really just like hearing the sound of their own voice bouncing off of you.

The Third point I want to make is in regards to Professionalism and Public Image. There is no substitute for Professionalism, none. How many times have you gotten terrible, unprofessional service at a Store/Restaurant and have vowed never to go back again? Hey, the food or goods may have been great quality b.u.t. because of the lack of service you received, maybe even on more than one occasion, you decided to not patronize this establishment anymore. Well, teaching Civilization is the same way. As Civilized People, we must always anticipate People's needs and exceed their expectations! This is the greatest service you can provide for someone, so it's important that we're Professional; or People will decide to never come back, AND tell many other People about how negative their experience was! Because of our standards of being those who have "*knowledge, wisdom, understanding, culture, refinement, and are not savages in the pursuit of happiness*", our job is 25/8 (not 24/7). We are not only on the Stage of Humanity, we set the Stage, and as The Fathers and Mothers of Civilization, People should always be able to look at us as models of Integrity and Wisdom. Even on our sick day we should be great! This means that our outward Public Image should coincide with the Principles and Values we inwardly subscribe to. What People cee on the outside should be synonymous with what's ticking on the inside. How we're living at Home should be a reflection of what we're doing Abroad. Everyone who claims to be God/Earth is an Ambassador of our Culture. If you're a Christian, Muslim, Buddhist, or etc.., you are an Ambassador of your Religion/Metaphysical System. What is the purpose of claiming something, that's supposed to help you become a better person, if you don't care how it effects (looks, feels, instructs, etc...) others? To me, this sounds like someone who wants the milk and no responsibility for milking the cow. It looks like a person who wants fulltime pay and benefits without being responsible for doing the work... Not only is it selfish, immature, and Egotistical, b.u.t. it's also completely inconsiderate to expect that People be receptive to any and everything we want to say/do (our Public Image), and then dismiss their thoughts/feelings about it by proclaiming, "I don't care what People think/say about what I do". Not only has this person closed themselves off from receiving any comments or constructive criticism that will be effective in helping them grow, b.u.t. they've put a great big sign on their back that reads, "please kick me!" Being aware of our Image and how we represent ourselves to the Public is only an advantage to us, and the lack of awareness or outright inconsideration of our Public Image will always be a disadvantage and eventually our demise.

In closing, I want to encourage all of us who claim to uphold the meaning of Civilization and duty of a Civilized Person to continue taking the higher road and being a beacon of light/life amongst our People and the Human Family as a whole. What we're saying/doing should matter first to the person in the mirror, and then this 'Consideration' must extend to our Family and Communities. By claiming Righteousness, we have taken upon the responsibility of adding our contributions to make this World a better place than when we got here. This is a Professional endeavor and demands the work of People who are unwilling to cut corners, take shorts, and do a half-ass job. That is unacceptable! This means that we must provide exceptional service to our People by anticipating their needs and exceeding their expectations of what being the True and Living Five Percenter, Christian, Muslim, Buddhist, or etc. is!

Building; a 'pro-action' word

The terminology "Building" has and is being used so loosely that I thought that it's important to clarify what this exactly means.

First and foremost, to "Build" means 'To Construct'. In the most simplistic terms: If the activities we're participating in are not Constructive, than that's a clear sign that we're not actually Building; it's Destroying. Why? Because we are not elevating our/anyone's thought process, way of approaching/assessing Life, and circumstances we/they are living in. As a matter of fact, if what we're conversing about is Constructive, then the evidence of it's application should be apparent in our people activities (how we're actually living). For example, if I'm talking about how the Black Man is God, then I shouldn't be in and out of Court/Jail for crimes I'm committing. If I'm calling myself a Queen, then my living environment or my attitude should not be a hovel.

Building is not an action word, it's a 'pro-action' word! To exemplify what "Building" means it requires that something is actually being done, Constructively. Many times I hear People talking about a lot of things, even in a highly intelligent way, b.u.t. nothing to very little in their day to day activities even remotely resembles what they're saying... Hey, we all have potential, b.u.t. all of us aren't doing something with it. When a person is actually Building, they realize that they're only as good as the last Project they completed, Knowledge they gained, and Skill they've acquired. They're constantly elevating, learning, and growing, and this is clearly evident in how they look, what they're doing, and how they're talking. Because they're being Constructive, the activities they're invested in are models for sustainability; they're not self important, materialistic, hedonistic pursuits because these things don't last! That's important to note because People may get the impression that someone is Building just because they're doing something... Let me emphasize again that it must be Constructive: elevating our/anyone's thought process, way of approaching/assessing Life, and circumstances we/they are living in. This is not because I say so, b.u.t. because these requirements dictate the nature and function of Building. In other words, what we're doing endures because it stands the test of time, tension, and integrity. An example of this is a Relationship that's Built upon the Principle of Love; it endures!

Although People may be under the impression that this terminology means "Conversing with another person", that is not entirely accurate. Building is not about what you're saying, pontificating, the rhetoric being spewed, lingo that's flipped & bounced, intellectualizing, or heated debates. The real emphasis is on how we've done or are doing what we're saying, AND how this has been instrumental in elevating our/anyone's thought process, way of approaching/assessing Life, and circumstances we/they are living in. Building is not Cellphone Philosophizing, Blog Boastin', or Fakebookin'... AKA 'Ghosts in the Shell'! Building also isn't sterile rants & raves about Academic Achievements in Mathematics/Science that lack a clear plan of action of how to use, and how WE ARE actually using these Achievements to better our Families, Community, and People. When I say "I'm Building!" then I should have something to actually show for it, literally. If we're studying Lessons/Scripture, then our life should demonstrate what we actually learned from that Lesson/Script, literally! The purpose of our study is not a philosophical exercise to talk about some historical events, or to show eachother how smart we are about something that clearly has nothing to do with why we still haven't started our own business/got a job, we're no step closer to being in a Relationship, our Attitude/Behavior in handling situations has not matured, or we're still holding on to a nasty habit that's actually killing us. We need to be more committed to eliminating the contradictions between what we say and what we're actually doing or not doing. We need to be more dedicated to growth & development than just reading a few pages of a book every other day, surfing the net to check out some things we're curious about, or using People to feel motivated. If we're going to Build then we need to be Constructive and stop procrastinating with our Life! Set short/long term Goals that are realistic and achievable, and work EVERY DAY to make them a reality while we're doing what's real. No that last sentence wasn't a typo! Lol I made sure to state "while we're doing what's real", because many of us may find ourselves waiting on that train to come in, long suffering until we die and go to heaven, or believing that one day in the future everything is just going to work out for us WHILE completely neglecting the work reality of today and our present-date resources and circumstances. At the end of each day, we should be taking Inventory of the quality of time we invested –which we will never get back. While assessing the quality of this time, we should be able to clearly cee and articulate how we've used it to elevate, learn, and grow. I'm not talking about using Supreme Mathematical tricks to try to rationalize a mediocre, mundane existence, or making Religious/Astrological abstractions in order to spice up a bland, flavorless lifestyle. I'm talking about being able to identify/demonstrate how we've literally elevated our/anyone's thought process, way of approaching/assessing Life, and circumstances we/they are living in.

In closing, I challenge all of us to begin TODAY by honestly taking an Inventory of our day before we go to rest tonight. Consider what you actually did to elevate your/anyone's thought process, way of approaching/assessing Life, and circumstances you/they are living in. Ask yourself how you were actually an asset to your Family, Community, and Society as a whole, and how you were a liability (procrastination? apathy?). Make a plan of 'pro-action' for tomorrow of how you are (not wish, hope, or want to) going to improve how you invested your time today, and commit yourself to it. If we're going to be a Builder than lets be that for real, and we can start by actually doing something Constructive today.

How to **MEET** our obligations

I'm driving pass the local High School recently just as Summer School was letting out and it looked like a regular School Day. I couldn't believe how many children were registered! As a form of general conversation I often ask the youth I come into contact with, "Are you going to Summer School?" and many of them shamefully say, "Yes", usually for Math, Science, and Language Arts. Through one of my close Associates who works for the School District, I also learned that many youth were turned down for Summer School because too many were already registered. Now what surprised me most was the large number of youth who are in Summer School this year for... drum roll... Gym. Yeah, that's right "GYM"! Who fails GYM?! If the only thing you're passing in School is 'The Office' so you can go to Lunch, and then 'Gas' after you eat it, something is terribly wrong with that picture... Aside from the obviously low pay our Teachers get and the poor Curriculum, there's a serious level of apathy I cee in today's youth I didn't cee growing up. I mean, I'm sure some of us were apathetic because I, and my entire Science Class, went to Summer School in 8th Grade for fooling around all year. Yet I have never even fathomed the type of apathy that would have youth, who are not overweight, going to Summer School for Gym.

Anyway, this serves as one of our biggest challenges for us as Adults, yes even those of you who have taken the initiative to Home School "your" child(ren). Home Schooled children undoubtedly come into contact with other youth who go to Public, Private, and Charter Schools, and apathy is as catchy as pink eye at a daycare. So in otherwords, the youth are ALL of our responsibility regardless where we live it, and even if we don't have any children of our own. Part of our responsibility is to help encourage our youth to develop a greater passion for learning, growing, and utilizing the resources available to them to help shape "their" destiny -key word being "their". I mention "their" simply because if the youth cannot relate or cee a personal interest in it then it won't mean anything, even when it's the truth. The youth are the Ambassadors of the future whether they're prepared or not, and if we aren't actively making our contribution to help them solve present day problems, we're adding to future our problems. So how can we, as Adults, help them **MEET** the expectations of bringing about a greater World than the one we were given responsibility for keeping? Well here is a simple formula I want to encourage you all to apply with the youth, starting with the youth in your own Family, extending to your Community, and then elsewhere.

MEET

M - Make a commitment to be a part of the solution, not the problem. I'm sure many People could relate about the apathy amongst our youth b.u.t. how many of us are actually doing something about it? Are we really committed to cee our youth do better or content with ceeing them frustratingly on a quest for fire? Once our word is bond, that bond will be life, and we should be willing to give our life before our word shall fail, just like we do with anything else we feel/believe is important to us.

E - Examine the reasons for the apathy our youth are experiencing. This means to listen! As Adults many of us are so involved in talking at, talking above, talking around, and talking about our youth that we rarely take the time to actually listen to their concerns, which are legitimate I might add. Listening means taking the time to find out what they think, like, feel, cee, and believe WITHOUT adding our two cents, cutting them off, or telling them what to do. When was the last time you too the time to listen to an Artist who's lyrics they quote better than a Preacher quotes Bible verses? What was the last movie you went to cee that they counted the minutes, seconds, and hours down to when it comes out? How many times have you actually asked the youth about their day and what's going on with them and mean it? The Generation Gap we cee is really a Communication Gap, and until we learn how to listen, it will be impossible to (re)establish the relationships with our youth to help close this Gap. If we're honestly not listening to them, why should they listen to us anyway? We can't ask for what we're not willing to give...!

E - Explore goals/interests that you both share. This establishes a level of Social Equality because now you're no longer -total-strangers. If you both can't stand broccoli, watch WWE, enjoy reading, or didn't like how Bella treated Jacob on Twilight, or any number of things, that's common ground to build on! Because you've already started to really listen to what they think, like, feel, cee, and believe, now you've begun to be exposed to things you may have never heard about and even start developing a real interest in. My prejudicial opinion of Drake was that he was W.A.C.K. until my oldest Queen put me on to him; we bumped his Album all Summer a couple years ago. When I first heard about 'The Pack' Rapper named Lil B and his BasedGod Movement from some of the youth, I didn't hesitate to learn what this is about, and because I follow up with them about various things I obviously don't understand, they don't hesitate to teach me. Because I've learned to "preserve the best part for myself and not be concerned [not care] about the poor part" when it's appropriate, yes there are some things I've found that are in common with how I cee Life, and these are the things that have helped further solidify our relationship. Now when I cee other youth and talk with them about it, they welcome me as a Newborn, after of course they first look at me like, "Who initiated you into our Society?" Lol If there is no common ground, you can't build with anybody, especially the youth.

T - Think outside of your box for solutions. When it comes to addressing the apathy our youth have towards Self/Academic Education, and some things that our youth may think, like, feel, cee, and believe that aren't positive/productive, we have to be creative. We have to come up with solutions that are a Win-Win situation for us both. For example, one day one of my Queens tried to put me onto Nicki Minaj and instead of me throwing up, I told her she wasn't as nice as Lil Kim. Obviously she disagreed, so we pulled up Youtube on our laptops and went song for song between Nicki and Kim, critiquing both lyrics and technique. There were some songs Nicki got her on and others Kim won, yet that wasn't my determined idea. In time I discreetly began to sneak MC Lyte (whom she already knew about), Isis, Rage, Bahamadia, Heather B.,Yo-Yo (who she thought was super wack), Boss, and other MC's in there in order to expose her to other Female Artists. The Win-Win situation in this case was both of us considering something different; thinking outside of the box! How's that for creativity? Lol Sometimes we have to be even more creative than that, and the determined idea is to agree upon something you're both willing/able to live with. Some Adults go amongst the youth with this chip on their shoulder like it's all about what they're going to teach them - with no respect or consideration for their choice to listen and learn, just like we have. Just getting the youth to consider what you have to offer, just like them getting you to consider what they have to offer, is a huge accomplishment. This is a major contribution to closing the Communication Gap between Generations.

Before we can even strive to tackle the problems going on outside, we have to first address the problems going on inside. Summer School is only the out-side effects of problems going on inside our Families and Communities. Some of the apathy the youth have is simply a mirror reflection of our apathy as their Parents, Guides, Community Leaders, and Elders. If you're not passionate about something then the youth definitely won't be inspired by you. The reason I expressed the above formula (**MEET**) was to demonstrate how this is an interactive endeavor. Why? Because we grow together! And some of you probably thought that we'll solve these problems going on with youth within our Families/Communities by sharing wisdom from our front porch like robins feed baby birds. No, you may have to play video games, go sledding, play soccer, and do other things the youth do. If you're not committed to them, in action, why should you expect them to be committed to you? Once we've committed ourselves to helping our youth grow and develop, we'll better position ourselves to **MEET** a brighter future for us all. By becoming more involved in their lives, our lives, we will better equip the youth with the tools necessary to bring about change. So I challenge all of you to help and continue to help our youth grow into the responsible stewards of a future World. The more they cee and get the encouragement from us to do better, they will. You did!

Contradictions with True Self Identification

When a person comes into KOS (Knowledge of Self), we go through a process of reevaluating our Philosophies on Life. We begin to question ideas/beliefs we've held about God, Family, Relationships, Diet, Education, Entertainment, and everything else that represents one's way of life (Culture). As we reevaluate these Philosophies there are three things that happen to us:

1. We learn that there are some things in our Philosophy that are still valuable/true.

2. We learn that there are some things in our Philosophy that are no longer valuable/true.

3. We learn new Philosophies on life that are valuable/true that we may have never heard before or never considered much.

This reevaluation process brings us to a valley of decision each time we question an idea/belief. When we began to learn about the health issues that come along with eating pork and pork by-products, we had to make a decision about our diet.

Some of us stopped immediately, others took some time to stop consuming it, while others still chose not change their diet at all. Because this is a process, there are still ideas/beliefs People are dealing with that do not completely coincide with KOS, myself included, and these are called 'CONTRADICTIONS' (an incompatibility/inconsistency between two or more propositions). This is the importance of our reevaluation process and Building with one another; we are constantly learning the right ways to resolve these contradictions for the purpose of positive growth & development. In our lessons we learn that a small percentage (10%) of people, primarily Caucasians, represent the wealthy/elite within the Dominant Society we live in continues daily to teach the masses of People many of these contradictions in order to make - mental/physical- slaves out of all they can, so they can rob them and live in luxury. Because 'they continue daily' to inundate us with ideas/beliefs that contradict our Philosophy on Life, we are constantly in a state of psychological, socioeconomic, physiological, and agricultural warfare. There are two types of People who are dealing with these contradictions; those who are striving to do something about it, and those who're aren't striving to do something about it.

Those who are striving to do something about it are actively involved in ways to resolve what they honestly acknowledge as a contradiction. If they smoke cigarettes they'll be honest about what they've chosen to be addicted to and if they're not involved in some type of program, they'll be showing clear behavior/signs towards quitting. Those who aren't striving to do anything about it are still in love with these ideas/beliefs and don't want to give up these contradictions. If they smoke cigarettes they won't be honest about what they've chosen to be addicted to and won't be involved in any program or show any clear behavior/signs towards quitting. As a matter of fact they'll often try to justify why they do it by making illogical statements like, "*I'm not hurting anybody but myself*", as if they have no relationship/responsibility to a collective that will be effected by their sickness or physical death, "*I do what I want in my own Universe*", again, as if they have no relationship/responsibility to a collective that will be effected by their choices, and "*Just because I smoke, it doesn't make what I'm saying not true or me any less of a God!*", which is essentially right & exact, because it doesn't make what they're saying untrue, it makes them untrue for choosing to justify doing the complete opposite. While the former perspective of doing something about our contradictions is a natural part of growing up, and the reason why we Build with eachother, the later perspective of not doing something about it is not natural, and the reason why we Destroy.

One of the biggest contradictions I cee, particularly amongst Gods and People who claim to identify themselves with/as The Supreme Being, is how they also hold fast to Philosophies like "I'm only human", "No one is perfect", "That's just how I am", "You made me do it", "We all fall short or make mistakes", "I can't", etc... Either we truly cee ourselves as having no limitations with infinite potential (Supreme), or deep down inside we really believe we're only human and everybody makes mistakes. Either we have this Supreme ability to rise above and respond to any circumstance, or we don't! Those who are still secretly in love with ideas/beliefs that contradict a Godly Perspective, become Cultural traders; trying to use illogic, justifications, and rationalizations to make interpretations of what clearly doesn't coincide with this way of life. The bottom line is this: Regardless of what we're into or may choose to do that is a contradiction towards growth & development, are we striving to Build or Destroy, Elevate or Degenerate?

In regards to proper Identification, once we decide to identify our Self with/as The Supreme Being, there are certain ideas/beliefs we can no longer accept as true, and contradictions we cannot live with. Why? Because certain ideas/beliefs reflect the mentality and procedures of someone who doesn't identify themselves with/as The Supreme Being. If you're really The Supreme Being, then how can somebody "make you" mad or make you do anything for that matter? If you're really The Supreme Being, then how can you claim to be a Libra and that's just how you are? If you're really The Supreme Being, then how exactly do you, The Supreme Being, actually have flaws and make mistakes? None of this adds up and there is no way to reconcile any of these Philosophies because they completely contradict eachother. On one hand we claim to have unlimited access to all Omnipotence and Omniscience, yet on the other hand we're claiming to be only human.

In closing, I want to encourage those who are reading this to be diligent in reevaluating the words/concepts we use because many of them reinforce ideas/beliefs that completely contradict how we claim to cee ourselves. For People who don't subscribe to the idea that they are the True & Living God, it's fine for them to make declarations like "We all make mistakes" and "Nobody's perfect". That directly coincides with how they cee themselves. B.u.t. for us, that's not alright. If we subscribe to the idea that we are the True & Living God, then we don't make mistakes. We make choices that may not have been the most allwise, right & exact. Therefore, we do not accept mistakes as who/what we essentially are; they're learning Lessons to show forth and prove our power to transcend them. Why? Because we are essentially perfect; undiluted, mixed, or tampered with in any 'form' [circumstance]. Therefore, we do not accept the idea/belief that "Nobody's perfect"; every situation we're faced with is a perfect opportunity to demonstrate how we can rise to the occasion because the limited conditions [circumstances] we are temporarily going through can never be Supreme over us!

www.ingramcontent.com/pod-product-compliance
Lightning Source LLC
Chambersburg PA
CBHW071359280526
45787CB00001B/386